Las Vegas on the Dime

An Insider's Guide to Great Values

Las Vegas on the Dime

An Insider's Guide to Great Values

Michael Toole

JOHNSTON
ASSOCIATES
INTERNATIONAL

P.O. Box 313
MEDINA, WASHINGTON 98039
(206) 454-7333

Las Vegas on the Dime
First Edition

ISBN 1-881409-27-9

Cover design, production, typesetting, and layout by Kate Kilpatrick

Although diligent efforts have been made to confirm the accuracy of information contained in this work, neither the publisher nor the author is responsible for errors or inaccuracies or for changes occurring after publication. This work was not prepared under sponsorship, license, or authorization of any business, attraction, park, person, or organization described, depicted, or discussed herein.

Johnston Associates International
Post Office Box 313
Medina, Washington 98039
(425) 454-3490; FAX: (425) 462-1335; e-mail: jasibook@aol.com

Printed in the United States of America

Library of Congress Cataloging-in-Publication Data

Toole, Michael, 1968-
Las Vegas on the dime / Michael Toole.– 1st ed.
p. cm
Includes index.
ISBN 1-881409-27-9
1. Las Vegas (Nev.)–Guidebooks. I. Title

F849.L35 T66 2001
917.93'1350434–dc21

Contents

Dedication

This book is dedicated to the following people for their positive comments and encouragement in writing this book: Chiyoko, Karen, Duffy, James, Steve, Jay, Ginger (aka Ms. Vegas), Tony (an awesome drummer), Paul (I'll do a book on Boston soon), and finally — Sabrina – may you rest in peace.

Introduction

Las Vegas is the biggest tourist attraction in the country and one of the biggest in the world. Competition among the hotels to give you the best facilities, service, and entertainment has become so intense that it's worth your time to visit this unique city. Tourists from all over the world have learned that this city knows how to entertain. It was built virtually around the myth of a "gambler's paradise in the oasis." It's a city that stresses more is best, be it excitement, money, music, lights, dancing, or any other kind of indulgence you might imagine.

While these might be dubious merits, aren't you the least bit curious how much willpower you can exercise under these circumstances? Isn't this one of the reasons you're thinking about choosing Las Vegas as a vacation destination? The watchword here is *vacation*, so everyone should experience this "giant playpen for adults" at least once.

Las Vegas on the Dime is a budget guide that, like others you may be familiar with (Berkeley, Let's Go, Time Out, etc.), encourages you to explore beyond the most popular sights and events. You will gather interesting tales, meet like-minded people, discover different aspects to a city you thought you knew, and, most importantly – *save money*.

Las Vegas on the Dime doesn't downplay the fact that you are probably going to Las Vegas to experience the Strip in all its glorious neon. You'll find plenty of information in this book on what rides, dining places, and shopping areas won't sink your wallet – on the strip and in surrounding areas.

Las Vegas has a reputation for excessiveness in a lot of

things – gambling, food, alcohol, and sex. It has an overall ambiance of enormous vitality. It's a 24-hour town that does not know when to stop selling. On the downside, it's trapped itself into a marketing rut. After all, there is more to Las Vegas than casinos, expensive stage shows, greasy buffets, and tacky paraphernalia like a pair of dice clocks or a Tom Jones beer mug. I've met plenty of travelers eager to learn what else Las Vegas might have to offer. Vegas is one of the fastest growing cities in the United States, with over 5,000 new residents arriving every month. Surely they are doing more than working and playing in the casinos.

Being an avid travel addict fortune enough to explore much of the United States and parts of Europe, I know how handy it is to have a guide book that covers all the essentials of budget travel: cheap lodging, good dining, inexpensive ethnic markets, cool cafes, etc., that travelers should know about. Another intention of *Las Vegas on the Dime* is to encourage you to explore avenues outside the usual Vegas attractions by offering tips to some great values.

Las Vegas on the Dime touches on some of the lighter aspects of this intense city. You probably didn't come to Las Vegas to buy a discount CD, or go to an Ethiopian restaurant. However, knowing that these *are* available and that there just might be some other activities besides gaming, broadens any pre-conceived notions you might have about Las Vegas. Plus, when you stray off the strip and venture into some of the surrounding neighborhoods, you can meet some of our interesting citizens. What makes Vegas unique is that a hodgepodge of people from all over the world have settled here for a new life. Brooklyn, Chicago, Anchorage, Honolulu, Detroit, Toronto, Vancouver, Liverpool, Tokyo, and

Saigon are just a few of the cities of origin for these transplants. The baker of a pastry shop down the block from my house is from Sofia, Bulgaria. If you are a *true* budget traveler, people watching will be part of the fun.

Keep in mind that I am just one person. What's listed in the following pages are places that I've frequented for a very long time and have always offered me a great value, whether it's a good meal, a good buy, or good entertainment. Locals in this city like to claim that they know more about Vegas than anyone else. That's one of the neat things about a book like this – it challenges other people to contradict me, and results in some good information (whether about an eatery, clothing store, etc.) for future editions. So by all means, if you discover other hot spots and great deals, share the wealth and let me know!

Also, please consider that it's impossible for a travel guide to be completely up-to-date when the book hits the stands. Information such as the price of a roller coaster ride, or the active hours of a bookstore, may have changed. This book is meant as a reference guide, and nothing is set in stone.

I hope this book will help you find some bargains, give you some ideas for your itinerary, and encourage you to strike out on your own when you discover how accessible this city really is. Ultimately, I'd like this book to help you achieve something that every budget traveler wants from a vacation – to feel uninhibited in exploring anything you want, without worrying about the financial after-effects when it's done. So please, for my sake, have a blast!

Chapter 1

Getting Here and Around Town

Arriving By Air

Finding cheap flights to Las Vegas is seldom a problem. An excellent source for discounted airfares can be found on the Internet. If you're a student who is too poor to afford a computer, let alone an Internet service, go to your University and ask if you can set up an account. It will be worth it. Getting deals on the net can save up to 60% off your airfare.

If you're a seasoned traveler, then you probably know that an APEX (Advance Purchase Excursion) ticket can be fairly inexpensive when purchased by a travel agent or directly from the airline. Depending on the airline, these tickets must be purchased in advance of the flight date, normally between seven to fourteen days. However, there is a downside. If for any reason you have to cancel the flight, it'll cost you anywhere from $50 to $75 to reschedule. Almost every major airline to Las Vegas has a website, and through these websites you can enter all the information required (number of passengers, date of departure and arrival, non-smoking, etc.) to acquire an apex ticket. Following are some of the Internet addresses of airlines that serve Las Vegas. I've also listed the toll free numbers for those of you who don't have access to the net yet (what's keeping you)? All of the airlines listed allow you to purchase tickets online — just begin with the familiar www.

alaska-air.com (800-252-7522)
americawest.com (800-235-9292)
flycontinental.com (800-523-3273)
delta-air.com (800-221-1212)
lufthansa.com (800-645-3880)
nwa.com (Northwest, 800-225-2525)
renoair.com (800-736-6247)
iflyswa.com (Southwest, 800-435-9792)
twa.com (800-221-2000)
ual.com (United, 800-241-6522)
americanair.com (800-433-7300)
frontierairlines.com (800-432-1359)
usairways.com (800-428-4322)
nationalairways.com (888-757-5387)

> This is probably as good a time as any to mention that all the local phone numbers listed in this book have a **702** area code. This is not just for Las Vegas, but for all of Clark County – which also include the cities of Henderson, North Las Vegas, Boulder City, Laughlin, and other Southern Nevada getaway stops.

If you're traveling by air, then you'll arrive at the **McCarren International Airport, 5757 Wayne Newton Blvd (261-5211).** You have several options of leaving the airport. Taking a cab isn't such a bad idea if you're traveling with at least two other people. Cab rides from the airport have a $1.20 departure fee, a $2.20 first mile fee, and a $1.50 cost for each additional mile. From McCarren to anywhere on the strip or downtown can cost you between $9-$18. If you split the fare between two other people, it's only $3-$6 per person (but don't forget to tip) and they'll get you there in a hurry! For more information, call the two local cab services: Whittlesea (384-6111) and Yellow (873-2227).

Shuttle service is for those traveling with a lot of luggage. There are a few services worth mentioning; however I should warn that you some of my friends have complained that these shuttle vans can be a tight squeeze. Shuttle services make their money by head count, so they really pack 'em-in. What's worse is that you ride with your luggage, making the ride more uncomfortable, particularly when it's a hot day because the air conditioning doesn't circulate too well in such close quarters.

Bell Trans (739-7990) – Charges $3.75 per person to any hotel or motel on the strip, $5 per person for the downtown area.

Gray Line (384-1234) – Charges $4 per person to any hotel or motel on the strip for one way. $5 per person for the downtown area for one way.

CLS Trans (740-4545) – Charges $4 per person to any hotel or motel on the strip, $5 per person for the downtown area.

Las Vegas Limo (739-8414) – Charges $3.75 per person to any hotel or motel on the strip, $4.75 for the downtown area.

Star Trans (646-4661) – Charges $4 per person to any hotel or motel on the strip, $5 per person for the downtown area.

The best idea if you are traveling lightly (i.e. no more than two carry-on items or one big suitcase) is to take the **Citizen's Area Transit (CAT)** bus service. There are two bus lines that leave McCarren: Paradise (108), or Maryland (109*). Both bus lines are located on the ground level at the north end of the terminal and will take you all the way to the Downtown Transit Center (DTC), where a majority of your inexpensive lodging can be found. If you need to transfer to the strip, take the 108 (Swenson – 30 minutes). The service isn't as frequent as the 109 (Maryland – 15 minutes), but the buses are *a lot less crowded.* The 109 line runs through one of busiest shopping streets on the eastside of town, whereas the 108 line runs through a residential district – hence the difference. Also, the 108 line is a few blocks closer to the strip, saving you a few minutes in the process.

*see page 18

Driving to Las Vegas

If you don't like to fly, then driving to Vegas is a good option. It couldn't be simpler. If you're coming from Utah or Southern California, take the I-15. If you're coming from Texas or New Mexico, take the I-10 west to Phoenix and the U.S. 93 (Boulder Highway) into town. Finally, if you're coming from Northern California, take I-80 east to Reno and then take U.S. 95 south; from here it's a straight (albeit boring) shot to Las Vegas.

Arriving By Bus

So you don't have a car? Take the bus — it's always a cheap option. Taking a Greyhound into town has been the last salvation for many a desperate soul trying to make good for him or herself in Vegas. Consequently, traveling by bus – especially in the neighboring states – remains a very affordable option.

The **Greyhound Bus Terminal** is located downtown on **200 S. Main Street, 382-5468, www.greyhound.com**, one block from Jackie Gaughn's Plaza Hotel & Casino, and is near the DTC. When the bus pulls in, you can walk to the DTC bus terminal within five minutes. Just ask any of the bus attendants for directions.

Getting Around Vegas By Bus

There is an information booth inside the Downtown Transit Center (DTC) where you can get bus route information **(228-7433; Hours: 6:15am – 9:45pm, Mon-Fri; 6:15am**

– 5:45pm, Sat, Sun & Holidays); www.rtc.co.clark.nv.us/cat/cat.htm. It's better *not* to direct your questions to the bus drivers who are on their break inside the DTC terminal. They embrace their breaks fervently and sometimes the more irritable bus operators won't be too helpful when you approach them during this time. Besides, most will only point you to the information booth anyway.

Bus fare is $1.25 and transfers are free. The exception are the strip buses (the 300 lines: 301*, 302*, and 303*), these lines are $2. The fares are good for one way, so you cannot use the transfers on the same bus line for a return trip. If you plan on using public transportation for a good part of your stay, then it would be wise to purchase bus tokens. A bag of 40 will cost you $22.50. At two tokens per trip you can get 20 trips out of this bag of tokens and save 25%. The best thing about the tokens is that they don't expire, so you can use them when you come back to Las Vegas for your next visit. Unfortunately, CAT does not offer a weekly discount pass, only a 30-day pass. If you find yourself staying here for that length of time, then it's a very good value. You'll get unlimited rides for a month for just $30. For more information, write to the **Regional Transportation Commission of Clark County, 301 E. Clark Avenue, #300, Las Vegas, NV 89101 (228-7433).**

> An asterick * after a bus line number (i.e. 109*, 206*) means that the route runs 20 minutes or less. This way you can plan your time wisely with the routes that offer the most frequent service.

Another public transportation service that's a little more expensive services only the tourist spots. **The Las Vegas Strip Trolley, P.O. Box 15333, Las Vegas, NV 89114 (382-1404),** charges $1.50 (one-way, and they're sticklers for the exact amount), and you can ride anywhere on the strip or downtown and even circulate among some of the local malls. The Trolley run begins at the DTC every day between 9:30 am and 2 am, and leaves the DTC every 20 minutes. This is your one chance to get a feeling of old San Francisco on the Las Vegas Strip.

The Weather

For many tourists, the weather tends to be of secondary importance since they spend most of their time indoors gambling. Even if that applies to you, you will be walking the strip or waiting at a bus stop, and you should have an idea of what the weather will be like so you can dress accordingly. Here in the southwest we love our desert climate, because the temperatures are generally moderate — especially when you compare us to other cities like New York or Chicago, the hometowns of a majority of our most recent residents. In the winter, be prepared for temperatures between 45F - 65F, and dress accordingly. April and May are arguably Las Vegas's best months weather-wise. Temperatures seldom rise above the high 80s and there is just enough of a desert breeze to cool you off if you've taken in too much sun. The months of June through September can make for some pretty intense afternoons. The dry desert heat can take a lot out of you as it hits highs of 116F and *hotter*, so bring plenty of bottled water, moisturizer and sunscreen. The fall season from October though the Christmas holidays has been terrific in recent years. Temperatures with highs in the 70s were common, and many locals found themselves hiking, bike riding, or ballooning, making this *the* season for outdoor pursuits.

Rain is seldom a hassle in our city's arid climate. The average annual rainfall is only 4.19 inches. However, this relatively low number has given the city a slightly false sense of security. Las Vegas has never really implemented good flood control measures, so one should be especially cautious on the eastside of town, where some of the older roads have poor drainage and lack floodlines, making driving a difficulty. While this is only an occasional problem, keep an eye on the weather reports or call our local weather line, 248-4800.

Bank Cards, Checks and Currency Exchange

Bankcards are never a problem in this city. Every major hotel, casino, supermarket, or convenience store has an automated teller machine. ATM's will accept all the logos like Plus, Star, or Cirrus. These machines, as well as your bank, may charge you anywhere from $1-$3 for a transaction. Therefore, it's wise to take out more than the minimum $20 per transaction. **One strong note of caution:** the major hotels will have some ATMs that belong to a system known as instant-teller. Avoid this. It exploits those who are in desperate need of quick cash. They allow you to take money out of your credit card without a pin number, and then charge exorbitant fees for the transactions. Taking out a mere $50 can cost you up to $9 for the service!

The transient nature of Las Vegas makes this a difficult town to cash personal checks. Some of the major hotels have a very guarded policy on this. A better idea is to take advantage of the numerous check-cashing businesses that are all along the Strip and Downtown area. These places will handle out-of-state personal checks, money orders and even savings account passbooks. Naturally, verification with one or two forms of personal identification is required, and there might be a fee, but a small one. Once your check is approved you are given another check, written and guaranteed by the check cashing company. The casino should cash it (providing you have proper ID), any time of day or night. And if worse comes to worse, there's always **Western Union, 800-325-6000).** Call the 800-number for a location near you.

There aren't too many places to recommend if you're trying to exchange foreign currency. The Bureau De Change at the McCarren Airport is a rip-off, charging you as much as 15% of what you're selling. The best bet in town is the **Foreign Money Exchange, 3025 Las Vegas Boulevard South (737-7803).** They offer the top exchange rates with no service fee. They buy and sell over 75 foreign currencies, accept foreign bank and government checks and even have a foreign wire service. There's a minimum $20 purchase for all foreign currencies and if you're selling foreign currency; only paper notes will be bought. **Bus Lines** 112, 301*.

Medical Services

I hope that your stay in Vegas won't come to this, but it's always a good idea to know where the major hospitals are just in case of an accident. There are two main hospitals in the center of town that offer around-the-clock emergency services: **University Medical Center, 1800-W. Charleston Boulevard (383-2000)** and **Sunrise Hospital and Medical Center, 3186 Maryland Parkway (731-8080)**. If you happen to be on the northwest side of town, the hospital that serves 24-hour emergencies is **Mountain View Hospital, 3150 N. Tenaya Way (869-9200). Bus Lines:** UMC - 206*, SHMC - 109*, 112, Mountain View – 211, 218.

Car Rentals

Given that we have a fairly decent bus system, car rentals are mostly useful if you want to go on a short getaway trip, or cover a lot of ground in a limited time. Almost all the major rental chains require you to be at least 25 years of age and possess a major credit card. Keep in mind that car rentals within a one mile radius of the airport have an additional 10% tax, so do your homework. A majority of these agencies have toll free numbers and websites:

Budget Rent a Car, 800-327-9633, 736-1212, www.budgetrentacar.com

Dollar Rent A Car, 800-800-4000, 739-8408, www.dollarcar.com

Payless Rent-A-Car, 800-729-5377, www.800-payless.com

Practical Rent-a-Car, 800-722-7209, 798-5253

Hertz, 800-654-3131, 736-4900, www.hertz.com

Thrifty Rent A Car, 800-367-2277, 896-7600, www.thrifty.com

U.S. Rent-a-Car, 798-6100

Value Rent A Car, 800-468-2583

Rent A Wreck, 800-227-0292, 474-0037

X-Press Rent-a-Car, 800-795-2277, 795-4008, www.xpressrac.com

Alamo, 800-327-9633, 263-8411, www.freeways.com

National, 800-227-7368, 261-5391, www.nationalcar.com

Avis, 800-230-4898, 261-5595, www.avis.com

Savmor, 800-634-6779, 736-1234

Airport Rent-a-Car, 800-631-8909, 795-0800

Resort Rent-a-Car, 800-289-5343, 795-3800

Special Events

Some of our special events are worth looking into ahead of time so you can plan your trip accordingly. The choice of activities is so varied, and at times has such a cross-section of appeal, that it might be easier to list the whole spectrum of events that are consistently popular in Las Vegas.

Due to our strong Asian population, we have one big, consolidated event that represents the better aspects of Asian culture. The Chinese New Year is celebrated at the **Chinatown Plaza, 4125 Spring Mountain Road at Arville Road** and is an incredibly festive occasion. The Chinese New Year is in accordance with the Chinese lunar calendar (as of 2000 the New Year was February 5). During this period, local Asian merchants get together and throw the **Asian Food**

Festival. Held at the Chinatown Plaza, it costs $2 to get in and will get you some free food samples, but you'll have to pay various businesses and ethnic fundraisers for some substantial food. The good news is you won't pay too much. That's because these merchants sell their entrees at a low price, hoping that you'll seek out their business another day. Elsewhere, there are prizes (I won a geisha fan last year),

The World Series of Poker

Held at Binoin's Horseshoe, 128 Fremont Street, 382-1600. This three-week event gathers, as you might guess, the best poker players in the world. It all started as an eight-man contest in 1970 by Benny Binoin, a popular gambler and hotel owner, who shrewdly anticipated the publicity and media coverage such an event like the "World Series of Poker" would create. In the last 30 years, thousands of competitors from all over the world have participated in this tough, highly competitive event.

You can study all kinds of poker here: Seven Card Stud, Deuce to Seven Draw, Omaha High-Low Split, and the biggie — the No Limit Texas Hold 'em — the tune to which the big boys dance. The contests range from a $1500 buy-in to the main event — the $10,000 Texas Hold 'em, Buy-in World Championship.

Although all the contests are an interesting lesson in subtlety and skill, there is no dispute that the No Limit Texas Hold-'em is the contest that demands most of your music acts, tae kwon do demonstrations, and your chance to pose with a tiger ($5). There's also a string of vendors, selling everything from Mao Sae Tung key rings to books instructing you how to reach the spirit of Bruce Lee. See you there! **Bus Line:** 203.

Spike and Mike's Sick and Twisted Festival of Animation has been one of the coolest treats we've had in the city

attention. Held over a four-day period (often the final days of the event), the Texas Hold 'em is an amazing game of courage, judgement and card sense. In this particular brand of poker, the player reveals two cards as their remaining cards are hidden in the hole. The dealer reveals three cards simultaneously and the players bet. A fourth card is revealed and again they bet. The final card is revealed and the players either raise or fold. It's a fast, nerve-tingling game and grandly entertaining for the audience. Sure, it's great to have good cards, but with No Limit Texas Hold 'em there is *no limit* to what the players can raise with their chips, so it's possible to win the contest without ever holding a good hand.

Herein lies the fun: this contest relies on bluffs and reads, and you can watch a group of skilled, high-stake gamblers compete for a million dollars and study every nuance of gestures as they try to outmaneuver each other and go for the big pot. This event is normally held from the last week of April to the first two weeks of May. **Bus Lines:** 108, 205.

for the past five years. Held at the **Huntridge Performance Arts Theater, 1208 E. Charleston Boulevard at Maryland Parkway, (477-7703), www.Huntridgetheatre.com,** it contains adult fare (you must be 18 years or older), with such alluring titles as "Jurassic Fart", "Little Rude Riding Hood", and the ever trendy "Hut Sluts". Some of the film animation is cell, some clay, and some computer graphics. In terms of quality, it's a wildly mixed bag. The films range from the sophomoric and repetitive to the savagely witty and original. Harry Crumb would certainly be interested to see what his spiritual disciples are doing! It's held during the final weeks of February or early weeks of March and ticket prices are only $7. **Bus Lines:** 109*, 206*.

On the third weekend in September is the **Festival of Greek Food.** This food feast is held at **St. John Greek Orthodox Church, 5300 El Camino Road at Hacienda Boulevard (248-3896).** This wonderful get together is a real cultural insight into Greek customs with music, dancing and delicious food. There's also — you guessed it — a raffle. Among the food specialties: lemon chicken, pastitsio, beef souvlaki, and much, much more. There's even an open-air marketplace that sells spices, produce and other ingredients characteristic of Greek food. General admission is $2, dinners are $10, the non-alcoholic drinks an additional $1.50, and wine and beer $2-$4. There's also a dessert section with more baklava and other baked goods than you could possibly imagine. You can buy a coupon book with up to $5 worth of discounts for any of the aforementioned foods. A raffle ticket included in the coupon book features prizes like a free trip to Hawaii, or a 25" color television set. This event has been held every year since 1973 and attendance increases every year! **Bus Lines:** 102, 201*, walk down two blocks south of Tropicana Avenue.

Right on the heels of the Greek festival, on the second weekend of October, the **Rio Hotel All Suite Casino Resort, 3700 W. Flamingo Road at Valley View off I-15 (247-7895, the event hotline)**, holds a popular event known as the **Italian Food Festival.** There are spaghetti eating and grape stomping contests, marionette shows, flag wavers from Italy, a lottery drawing and some great food like pizzas, calzones, cheeses, and assorted pastas. Admission into the festival is free, and it's up to each booth to charge for their food samples, but it's inexpensive. **Bus Line:** 202*.

Comdex is one of the biggest conventions Las Vegas has all year. Hotels, restaurants and tour groups are booked to the nines during this time. With the exception of New Year's Eve, merchants rarely get this excited about all the possible business. The Comdex show features the latest in computer technology. Although it's expensive to get in (tickets start at $75), die-hard computer junkies swear it's worth it. It's held every Mid-November at the **Las Vegas Convention Center, 3150 Paradise Road (892-0711). Bus Lines:** 108, 112.

The National Finals Rodeo attracts droves of cowboys. This 10-day event is held at **UNLV's Thomas and Mack Center, 4505 Maryland Parkway (895-3900).** The best bronco riders and clowns compete and strut their stuff in this truly amazing western spectacle that draws over 175,000 spectators. I should warn you that tickets go on sale for the next year's finals immediately after the event is over, so call the Thomas and Mack Center for further details. Held at the end of November every year. **Bus Lines:** 108, 201*.

Finally, we have our **New Year's Eve** celebrations. The strip is closed off from Sahara Avenue to Hacienda Boulevard (a stretch of 2.5 miles) for revelers to walk and absorb that feeling of reckless abandon, drunken celebration and bad kareoke singing (it's fun to me). Enjoy any of the rollercoaster rides at the MGM or New York, New York resorts which are open until midnight on New Year's Eve. Grab some pizza, (Dominoes Pizza employees aggressively sell pizza on every block), watch some fireworks, and, with any luck, a hotel implosion (as in blowing one up!)

Another choice for a New Year's Eve celebration is the **Fremont Street Experience,** five blocks of coveted outdoor casinos and stores with an overhead light display located in downtown Las Vegas. There's a concert performance for the final evening of the year and Vegas revelers rang in 2001 with some fine 80s dance funk with bands like Kool & the Gang & The Gap Band, who created an inviting undercurrent that grooved the audience into unison. The evening's event costs $25 and it is crowded, but you'll have a chance to mingle with people from all walks of life, and whether they're intoxicated or not, it is a hoot. (800) 249-3559, (702) 678-5600. **Bus Lines:** The Strip: 108, and walk two blocks west to the strip, 301*, 302*, Downtown: 105, 106, 301*, 302*.

Publications and Radio

Publications exist to help you find out what's going on in the alternative scene around town. Just don't expect anything on the scale of New York's "Time Out" magazine. The following is a list of sources for information on band gigs, eateries, and assorted offbeat events that deliver fun with a difference.

City Life, P.O. Box 27409, Las Vegas, NV 89126-1409 (871-6780), www.lvcitylife.com. This paper does a valiant job in telling you all the latest gigs, hip nightspots, cool film festivals, and general buzz on what to do in the city. It's pretty campy too, with essays ranging from a night in a lowbrow motel, to the evolution and cultural acceptance of the Teriyaki Bowl. This magazine carries those ever-popular personal ads (man seeking man, man seeking woman, man seeking women with bisexual tendencies, etc.) so if you are in Las Vegas and alone, here's your chance to connect with someone. To a lesser extent, **The Las Vegas Weekly, P.O. Box 230657, Las Vegas, NV 89123-0011 (990-2420), www.vegas.com**, is widely considered to be the rival to "Citylife". The writing can be a little spotty, but they do a good job of researching some of the entertainment acts in town as well as the new musical acts in the city. Since the paper is free, why not give it a look?

The Las Vegas Press, 3335 Wynn Road, Las Vegas, NV 89102 (871-6780), might be useful for checking out coupons and entertainment listings. Also helpful will be the **Las Vegas Music Press, 516 Fremont Street, Las Vegas, NV 89101 (471-7625)**, that lists a majority of the city's music venues, from blues, jazz and salsa to classical. **Vegas Music**

& Film Magazine, 2692 Florence Avenue, Las Vegas, NV 89120 (736-3158), www.vegasmusicandfilm.com, has a huge calendar spread that lists every conceivable event and then some: lounge, kareoke, hypnotists, comics, record collectors, film festivals and so on. It's geared more for the fan of the local music scene than for the casual tourist.

On the more conventional side, try **Today in Las Vegas, 3626 Pecos-McLeod, #14, Las Vegas, NV 89121 (385-2737), www.todayinlv.com**, a useful magazine for good, ethnic restaurants. They also offer a slew of coupons for the strip shows. Our city newspaper, **The Las Vegas Review-Journal, 1111 W. Bonanza Road, Las Vegas, NV 89106 (383-0211), www.lvrj.com**, isn't quite so varied in its information, but once in a while casinos with new lounge acts of the dated "Cocktail Exotica" variety will throw in a discount coupon, and it's a great way to relive the cheesy grooves of yesteryear. The Review-Journal also produces an arts magazine published every Friday, **Neon Magazine, P.O. Box 70, Las Vegas, NV 89125, www.lvrj.com/lvrj_home/neon/**, that has the entire lowdown on many variety acts of both homegrown talent and those on tour.

Finally, check any of the visitor's bureaus for two valuable magazines. **Showbiz Weekly, 2290 Corporate Circle Drive, Suite 250, Henderson, NV 89014 (383-7185), http://showbiz.vegas.com** and the sleeker **What's On in Las Vegas, 4225 S. Industrial Road, Las Vegas, NV (891-8811, 800-494-2876), www.ILOVEVEGAS.com.** Although they are more conventional in their entertainment and restaurant reporting, they have discount coupons for many shows on the strip as well as 2-for-1 dining specials for various restaurants at some of the big hotels. All of these papers are free for one copy (which you can usually find in any coffee shop or bookstore in town), but if you want to subscribe it might cost you a minimal amount. Just write, call, e-mail, or check out the web sites at the sources above for more information.

Some of the alternative radio stations are worth the listen, if only to find what's going on in entertainment. **KUNV, 91.5 FM,** is UNLV's campus radio station and offers a mix of jazz, world music, reggae and even big band.

Finally, for those of you with a craving for interesting new restaurants in town you might want to check out the "A Taste of Las Vegas" program on **KNEWS 970 AM.** It's on every Saturday afternoon, between 3:05pm and 4:00pm. It's an offering for people with more upscale tastes, but since Las Vegas is a city where a restaurant can open or fold every week, it's a good idea to listen to some news and reviews just to keep up with what's happening in town.

Information Bureaus

The Las Vegas Convention and Visitors Authority, 3150 Paradise Road (800-332-5333, 892-0711), www.lasvegas24hours.com, is useful to get information like maps, upcoming attractions, special events or concerts.

The Las Vegas Chamber of Commerce, 3720 Howard Hughes Parkway, at Flamingo Road (735-1616), www.lvchamber.com, can provide similar information as above, but be sure to ask them for a publication called "Visitors Guide". It's a fine magazine, with plenty of info on what's up in the city, and it might even contain some coupons for upcoming attractions or shows.

Finally, here are some Chambers of Commerce for those who want to explore the culturally related events in our city.

Virtually every demographic segment of our city including Latino (which by the end of 1997, was calculated to have more than 160,000 residents in the city, making them the highest populated minority in Las Vegas), Asian, Jewish, Gay, and African American, are well represented by these organizations:

Urban Chamber of Commerce
P.O. Box 4850
Las Vegas, NV 89106
648-6222, www.ucworld.org

Latin Chamber of Commerce
829 S. Sixth Street
Las Vegas, NV 89101
385-7367, (website under construction)
Bus Lines: 107*, 301* (a block away from both stops)

Asian Chamber of Commerce
900 Karen Avenue
Las Vegas, NV 89109
737-4300, (website under construction)
Bus Lines: 109*, walk two blocks west

Jewish Community Center of Southern Nevada
3909 S. Maryland Parkway, Suite 400
Las Vegas, NV 89109
794-0090, www.jewishlasvegas.com
Bus Line: 109*

Gay and Lesbian Community Center
912 E. Sahara Avenue
Las Vegas, NV 89101
733-9800, www.thecenter-lasvegas.com
Bus Line: 204

Chapter 2

Accommodations

No matter where you go for a vacation, unless you can stay with friends or family, accommodations will always be a big percentage of your travel budget. Fortunately, Las Vegas has its healthy share of cheap lodging, but you must be careful where you stay.

The hotels in this city can fluctuate wildly with their room prices because the criteria for the rate adjustments is so convoluted that by the time you hang up the phone, you feel as disoriented as a freshly landed trout. The criteria *seems* simple: it depends on popular seasons (spring-summer), busy holidays (Thanksgiving or Valentine's Day), or if there's a particular convention in town. Yet it's not always as simple as that.

Having worked as the Research Coordinator for the monthly publication, "The Las Vegas Advisor", one of my responsibilities was to check out room rates for all the major hotels. I have made calls to hotels 30 minutes after a prior call, and the rates have shot up anywhere from $50-$100. Why did this happen? It can be due to any number of reasons: "A business group just made several reservations," or, "it was a special that just finished this past hour," and my favorite, "I don't know, but I'm sorry sir."

Don't mislead yourself into thinking any reasonably priced motel will necessarily be a good value. Some motels might offer great prices, but have an unsavory atmosphere. I was amazed at how some of the shadiest dives, often populated with derelicts, would quote me prices more expensive than some of the major hotels in town. Their sole "virtue" was that you get free porno flicks, and for that it's worth $99 a night for an off-season weekday? Even more aggravating are rude managers who will almost never give you a direct quote for a room over the phone.

Needless to say, these resting stops are not recommended in this book. If anything, these dives only strengthened my appreciation for the better lodgings that I visited. I found an endearing quality to them, particularly when I struck up conversations with other guests who were staying in nearby rooms.

Most importantly, the following recommendations for accommodations should be used as a starting point. Feel free to check out some of the major hotels, particularly *after* a major holiday. For example, during the first two weeks of January this year some of the new hotels (i.e. The Paris, MGM) had rates as low as $59 a night. These hotels have an average rate daily rate of over a $100 on weekdays and anywhere from $150-$200 on a weekend — and that's not necessarily during high season either. The hotels listed here are pretty consistent with room rates because they offer a rate set months in advance, with little or no fluctuation. The motels listed here are ones that I've stayed in and found to be a safe environment with decent furnishings and most importantly, were easy on the budget.

If you're staying for only a few days, keep in mind that almost all the major hotels and motels have their cheapest rates Sunday through Thursday. On Friday and Saturday, rates can go up anywhere from $15-$25 a night. It gets even worse from the Thanksgiving Day holidays through New Years Day by an additional 60%-120%, so if you plan on traveling during these busy holidays, you'd better call ahead to see what you can afford. All prices are marked for double occupancy and do not include tax. Room tax is 9 per cent south of Sahara Avenue (where the county line begins — you know it as the strip), it's 11 per cent if you're staying north of Sahara Avenue (consider this downtown).

The hotels on the strip and downtown will hold a room for you if you give them a major credit card. The smaller outlets like motels and hostels will most often have a first come, first serve basis. Still, it never hurts to call. It might be a particularly slow season, and depending on the manager you talk to, you just might get lucky.

Here's the key for the price breakdown:

$	(under $30)
$$	($30-$60)
$$$	($60-$90)
$$$$	(over $90)
*$w	(Discount if you stay over a week)

Here's the location key:

S	(Strip)
OS	(Off-Strip)
DT	(Downtown)
O	(Other)

Motels & Casinos

Circus Circus Hotel and Casino

2880 Las Vegas Boulevard South (800-634-6703, 734-0410), www.CircusCircus-lasvegas.com – This is Rosie O'Donnell's favorite hotel on the strip. Although her description of the Circus as the "Coney Island" of Las Vegas is a bit of a stretch, there's no denying that the live Circus acts at the midway (everyday from 11am to Midnight), the sprawling variety of arcade games, and the funky pink, white and blue pin-striped wallpaper (hey, those are Circus colors, give them credit for detail) all add an element of lowbrow funseeking that the other hotels lack. The key motive for most visitors is the bargains you get for the rooms. During the off-season, you can snare a room for as little as $40 a night on a weekday. Keep in mind that the cheapest rooms at Circus Circus are going to be the "motel-styled" rooms that are detached from the casino. However, it's less than a three-minute walk to the casino. **Location**: S. **Amenities**: Three swimming pools, cable TV, private bath, laundry room, phone for local calls, and – you're smack in the middle of the strip! **Credit Cards**: Visa, MasterCard, American Express and Discover. **Rates: $$**, Sun.-Thurs., **$$$**, Fri. and Sat. **Bus Lines**: 301*, 302*.

The Showboat

2800 Fremont Street at Boulder Highway (800-634-3484, 385-9123), www.showboat-lv.com – The oldest hotel/casino on Boulder Highway (built in 1954) is still warmly embraced by locals for two key reasons: the bowling alley and huge bingo parlor. Showboat also offers some very good room rate specials that can be as low as $29 a night on an off-season weekday. Another advantage to the Showboat is that it's very close to the downtown area — just a quick five minute drive. At the 106-lane alley hotel guests receive discounts. The alley is a popular stop on the PBA tour and although some of you might not consider bowling the most enthralling spectator sport, the intense national coverage by ESPN of the tournament (and the audience surrounding it) make it a fairly hip event. Showboat's bingo parlor seats over 1200 and offers some of the biggest payouts in town. **Location**: O. **Rates: $$**, Sun-Thurs; **$$-$$$**, Fri-Sat. **Amenities**: No frills, but includes a queen-size bed, night table, laundry facilities, cable TV and ample parking. **Credit Cards**: Visa, MasterCard, and American Express. **Bus Line**: 107, 206*.

Westward Ho

2900 Las Vegas Boulevard South at Desert Inn Road (800-634-6803, 731-2900), www.westwardho.com – Not the most exciting hotel on the strip, but very quiet if that's what you seek. The restaurants are average and you won't find headlining acts here. However, here you will find the most consistently cheap rooms on the strip. Located right between the Stardust and Circus Circus, the Ho (don't laugh, that's what we call it) has rates normally around $35 a night on a weekday and $45 on a weekend. Even during holidays and conventions, the rates are only slightly higher than that. Also, with 777 rooms, your chance for vacancy is pretty good. **Location**: S. **Amenities**: A clean bedspread, TV, laundry service, safety deposit boxes, and not much else. **Rates: $$**, Daily, **Credit Cards**: Visa, MasterCard, and American Express. **Bus Lines**: 301*, 302*.

Four Queens

202 Las Vegas Boulevard South (800-634-6045, 385-4011), www.fourqueens.com – Clean, reliable, accessible and almost always overlooked and undervalued, the Four Queens is tops on this author's list for a good room value. Situated in the Fremont Street Experience, feel free to shop at the inexpensive souvenir shops, or hit the cheap gambling joints that flood this area. I've been doing room rate research for nearly two years now and I've never seen the prices over $90 a night, even during high season (Christmas, Fall conventions, etc.). In off-season, rooms can often be as little as $25-$30 a night, and just $40 for the weekend – yes, these are motel prices, but with hotel/casino niceties. **Location**: DT. **Amenities**: The rooms are a bit tight, but with laundry services, cable TV, acceptable furnishings, room service and an attractive polish that comes with being a long-established, well-respected hotel in the downtown area. This is a real bargain. **Rates: $-$$**/Sun-Thurs, **$$-$$$**/Fri-Sat. **Credit Cards:** Visa, MasterCard, and American Express and Discover. **Bus Lines:** 301*, 302*.

Bourbon Street

120 E. Flamingo Boulevard, two blocks east from the Strip (800-634-6956, 737-7200), www.bourbonstreetlasvegas.com – This might come as a stylish surprise to some of you. Bourbon Street is a nine-story hotel that has over 166 rooms, a pleasing atmosphere and good accessibility to the strip — all of which makes it a strong candidate for the budget traveler. **Location:** OS. **Amenities:** Nice, spacious rooms upholstered in a pleasant burgundy, cable TV, laundry facilities, fax and copy service. Only drawback, there is no pool. **Rooms: $$-$$$**, Sun-Thurs., **$$$**, Fri-Sat. **Credit Cards:** Visa, MasterCard, and American Express and Discover. **Bus Lines:** 202*, 301*, 302*.

Tropicana Hotel

3801 Las Vegas Boulevard South (800-634-4000, 739-2222), www.tropicanalv.com – You have to tip your hat to the Tropicana. They have remained unfazed as other bigger, splashier hotels (New York, New York, Mandalay Bay) keep popping up around them, and while these mega-resorts might offer flash and ceremony, the humble Tropicana offers a friendly atmosphere, good rates, excellent location and well executed pastiche of history (their Casino Legends Hall of Fame has the largest collection of casino memorabilia ever assembled, with more than 700 casinos represented from the past 70 years). For budget lodging, request the garden rooms, which are located in three-story buildings detached from the casino. The walk to the hotel lobby is short, the rooms pretty spacious and the parking is very convenient. **Location**: S. **Amenities**: cable TV and a phone for free local calls, but pets are not allowed. **Rates: $$-$$$**, Sun-Thurs, **$$$-$$$$**, Fri-Sat. **Credit Cards**: Visa, MasterCard, American Express and Discover. **Bus Lines**: 201*, 301*, 302*

Las Vegas Club Hotel & Casino

18 E. Fremont Street at Main Street (800-634-6532, 385-1664), www.playatlvc.com — Generally acclaimed by every old-timer I've met as the first "themed" hotel/casino in the city (in this case, sports trivia). The LV Club has managed to maintain its old, streetwise, Vegas charm. You have to give this place credit; in a city where the nouveau riche want to tear down everything that's old and historic, the LV Club has been operating successfully since 1939! I'm not the biggest fan of sports memorabilia, but it's hard not to gape at the awesome collection the LV club has assembled (autographed footballs, uniforms and photographs), but it's the World Series bat collection (1946-1958), that gets my attention. There are over 400 rooms, so availability is seldom a problem. **Location**: DT. **Amenities**: Your choice of King or two Queen-Size beds, a night table, mini-sofa and a dresser. **Rates**: $$, Daily. **Credit Cards**: Visa, MasterCard, American Express and Discover. **Bus Lines:** 105, 207 (or any bus that takes you to the DTC, just walk to the Fremont Street Experience and head to the west end).

El Cortez Hotel

600 Fremont at 6th Street (800-634-6703, 385-5200), www.elcortez.com — A long-standing hotel located in the heart of downtown. The atmosphere surrounding the Cortez has been considerably more appealing in recent years since the city has made an earnest effort to clean up its downtown area. The recent edition of the "Fremont Street Experience," a coveted outdoor string of stores, casinos, and outdoor vendors with an overhead light display, has attracted more people, and the inclusion of a Las Vegas Metro Police substation down the block has added to the perception of safety. The El Cortez benefits from this since it is nearby. It's also very affordable and close to the Downtown Transit Center. If you don't have a reservation, check-in time is after 2pm. **Location**: DT. **Amenities:** You'll get the usual: a bed, TV, private bath, etc., but it's clean a room. **Credit Cards** - Visa, MasterCard, and American Express. **Rooms - $$,** Daily. **Bus Line:** 301*.

Golden Gate Hotel

1 Fremont Street, inside the Fremont Street Experience (800-426-1906, 385-1906), www.goldengatecasino.com – Las Vegas's oldest hotel was established in 1905. It's small even by downtown standards, but it *is* inexpensive and *is* in a dynamite location. The lobby is adorned with very old pictures of the hotel when it first opened, plus an occasional shot of the Golden Gate Bridge and Fisherman's Wharf, just to be consistent with its' namesake. There are 106 clean, simple rooms, with cable TV, your own phone to make free local calls, voice mail, and even a computer port. The best reason to stop in at the Golden Gate is for its celebrated 99¢

shrimp cocktails. Served at their Bar & Deli toward the back of the main floor, you'll get lots of ocean shrimp, a tangy cocktail sauce, and a wedge of lemon placed in a large tulip glass. It's a pretty popular hotel, so call ahead for reservations. **Location**: DT. **Amenities:** Pretty much what you'd expect, plus you get a great view of the Fremont Street Experience from your bedroom window. **Rates: $$,** Daily, **Credit Cards:** Visa, MasterCard, American Express and Discover. **Bus Lines:** 108, 205.

The Hotel San Remo

115 E. Tropicana Avenue at Koval Lane (800-522-7366, 739-9000), www.sanremolasvegas.com – Conveniently located among Las Vegas mega-resorts such as New York-New York and Excalibur, and sitting directly across from the MGM, the San Remo is an alternative to the impersonal hustle and bustle of the larger hotels but at a more affordable price. Apart from being a full-service casino with a few good restaurants, as well as a non-strip casino that has a tolerable lounge act, what's really attractive about this personal, relatively small casino is the mix of the guests. I mean, I've encountered them *all* here: cheerful mid-westerners, vocal New Yorkers, wandering cowpokes, European backpackers, hip collegiate types, attractive yuppie couples (both gay and straight), Persian and Japanese tour groups and even locals (we're a hybrid in ourselves), all come here and hang with one other quite comfortably. Like the Circus Circus, the cheapest rooms are "in the garden", which is detached from (but a quick walk to) the main casino. **Location**: OS. **Amenities**: A year-round heated swimming pool, room service, good lounge entertainment and an atmosphere that's uninhibited and unpretentious. Don't forget to check out their gaming lessons instructed in Japanese. **Rates: $$-$$$**, Sun-Thurs, **$$$-$$$$**, Fri-Sat. **Credit Cards:** Visa, MasterCard, American Express and Discover. **Bus Lines:** 202*, 301*, 302* (for the 300 lines, walk just two blocks east of the strip and you'll be there in a few minutes).

Vacation Village Hotel and Casino

6711 Las Vegas Blvd South (800-658-5000, 897-1700), www.vacationvillagevegas.com – If you want to be as far removed as you can be from all the glitz and high-tech pyrotechnics of the mega-resorts, then Vacation Village is for you. With its faux Southwestern décor and "fine" dining establishments (Denny's Restaurant and Roberto's Taco Shop are the 24 hour accessible eateries), the Village is in a league of its own. Let me assure you though, for a fine value, the Village can rarely be surpassed. Calling the location convenient is an understatement. You're just *minutes* from the following: McCarran International Airport, all the strip attractions, access to Interstate Highways I-15 & I-95 and a mere block from Belz Factory Outlet Mall. The Village offers very consistent rates except for the major holidays. So even during *high* season on a weekend, rates are seldom more than $75 a night. It's drawback (apart from the lounge acts) is that with only 307 rooms, and given its "insider's" popularity (maybe the major travel guides won't mention them, but almost every local recommends the Village to their friends) availability can occasionally be a problem. **Amenities**: A video arcade for the rambunctious kiddies, sportsbook, handicapped-accessible rooms, pool hall, complimentary airport shuttle (upon availability), two outdoor pools & spa, beauty and hair salon, check cashing and fax & photocopy services. **Location:** OS. **Rates:** $$, Sun-Thurs, $$-$$$, Fri-Sat **Credit Cards:** Visa, MasterCard, American Express and Discover. **Bus Lines:** 212, 216, 217, 301*, 302*, 303.

Silverton Hotel and Casino

3333 Blue Diamond Road (800-588-7711, 263-7777), www.silvertoncasino.com – For some of you, this might not be the ideal location (it's off I-15 and Blue Diamond Road), but the rock bottom rates for a nice hotel/casino will no doubt entice the *true* bargain lovers. The casino is pretty mellow and understated, but the staff is friendly, and they have a first-rate buffet and café. One other plus, if you're tired of driving to the strip, is that the 303 bus line stops right in front of the hotel to take you to Vacation Village. From here you just transfer to the 301* or 302* and you'll be there in no time. **Location:** O. **Amenities:** 300 spacious rooms, in-room coffee makers, full bathrooms, room service, good places to eat and, as they claim, "the softest of beds". **Rates: $-$$**, Sun-Thurs, **$$-$$$**, Fri-Sat. **Credit Cards:** Visa, MasterCard, American Express and Discover. **Bus Lines:** 301*, 302*, 303.

Motels & Hostels

Budget Inn

301 S. Main Street at Bridger Avenue (800-959-9062, 385-5560) – A very popular motel, with very decent rooms considering the price. The managers will hold a nightly room for you, but you'll have no luck reserving a weekly. They have over 80 rooms so availability is good. **Location:** DT. **Amenities:** cable TV (but no premium channels), phones for free local calls. **Rates: $$** Sun-Thurs., **$$$** Fri and Sat., ***$w. Credit Cards:** Visa, MasterCard, and American Express. **Bus Lines:** 108, 205.

Fun City Motel

2233 Las Vegas Boulevard South at Sahara Avenue (731-3155, 735-7643) – An excellent value that's right on the edge of the strip. Some great, inexpensive eateries and shopping values listed in this book are virtually within walking distance of this motel. Yes, there are the usual luxuries for a low-rent motel: A big queen size bed, a phone for free local calls, a swimming pool, cable TV, and a coin-operated laundry room. There's also nighttime security and a bus stop right on the sidewalk. Yet with only 87 rooms, and being much closer to the strip than the other motels, you might have trouble getting a room during the holidays. **Location:** DT. **Amenities:** As I mentioned in the entry above – the *usual* luxuries for a low-rent motel! **Rates: $$**, Sun-Thurs., **$$$**, Fri and Sat., ***$w. Credit Cards:** Visa, MasterCard, American Express and Discover. **Bus Lines:** 204, 301.

Holiday Motel

2205 Las Vegas Boulevard South at Sahara Avenue (735-6464, 735-0420) – A small, comfortable motel with one of the friendliest staffs in town. Rooms are a bit old and I've seen better carpeting, but once again, a good location and relative inexpensiveness compensate for those slight drawbacks. Amenities: cable TV (no premium channels) and a phone for free local calls, but pets are not allowed and they have no laundry facilities (there's a laundromat across the street). **Location:** DT. **Rates: $$**, Daily, ***$w. Credit Cards:** Visa, MasterCard, American Express and Discover. **Bus Lines:** 204, 301.

Days Inn

707 Fremont at 7th Street (800-325-2344, 388-1400), 4155 Koval Lane at Flamingo Road (800-634-6541, 731-2111), www.daysinn.com – This popular chain has many branches in the city, but your best bet (and cheapest) is to stay in either of the two listed above. The downtown branch (Fremont) is a real bargain. You'll get fresh daily linens, satellite TV (but no premiums), a queen-size bed, 24-hour security, a coffee shop that's a training ground for students of the culinary union, and a groovy pool on the third floor that's they claim is "bottomless", but in reality is just very d-e-e-e-e-p. The Koval Lane location (which is just two blocks east of the strip) is a little more expensive since it's closer to the action. They also have a few more perks than its downtown sister. You'll get all of the above mentioned accommodations, plus a jacuzzi, a 24-hour restaurant, a bar with a nightly jazz combo, and a small parlor casino in the lobby to cut your gaming teeth. Call ahead for the summer, since both these motels get booked pretty fast. **Location:** OS. **Amenities:** I stated them earlier, plus a certain comfort level that comes with staying at a national chain. **Rates:** *Fremont* - **$$,** Daily, Koval - **$$,** Sun-Thurs., **$$$,** Fri. & Sat. **Credit Cards:** For both – Visa, MasterCard, American Express and Discover. **Bus Lines:** Fremont – 107*, 301*. Koval – 201*, 213.

Golden Inn

120 Las Vegas Boulevard North at Ogden Street (384-8204) – A step above average for the motels in this area.They don't take reservations, but they tend to have more vacancies here than at other motels. You get your own phone and the bus stop is right outside. **Location:** DT. **Amenities:** cable TV with Showtime, a pool, a phone (50¢ per call) and pets are allowed with a $50 deposit. There's no laundry facility, but there's one down the road. **Rates: $,** Daily, ***$w. Credit Cards:** Visa, MasterCard, American Express and Discover. **Bus Line:** 301*.

Travel Inn Motel

217 Las Vegas Boulevard North at Fremont Street (384-3040) – "Just 98 steps to downtown". That's what they advertise on the back of the building, and while those 98 steps depend on your stride, it is a superb location. You can walk to the Fremont Street Experience, catch the bus (it's right on the doorstep) to head to the strip, or drive straight onto Boulder Highway and Hoover Dam (Highway 95 South is just a heartbeat away). **Location:** DT. **Amenities:** The singles have a king-size bed, cable TV with HBO, a pool, a phone (50¢ per call), and pets are allowed with a $50 deposit, but there's no laundry facility. The furnishings are slightly above par (for a downtown motel) so it's a little costlier than most. **Rates: $**, Daily, ***$w; Credit Cards:** Visa, MasterCard, American Express and Discover. **Bus Line:** 301*.

Normandie Motel

708 Las Vegas Boulevard South at Gass Street (477-0144) – The oldest motel in the valley (est. 1928) is also one of the coolest places to spend a few nights. Elvis slept here in 1959. His ghost apparently haunts Room 1 (hey, it's good for business). Even if you don't get that room, don't worry, there are hand-painted pictures of him on the walls of the other rooms if you want to relate to the King's spirit. **Location**: DT. **Amenities**: All rooms have two queen size beds, Satellite TV, a phone for free local calls, recently reupholstered carpeting, and pets are allowed, but sorry, there is no pool or laundry facility. **Rates: $**, Sun-Thurs, **$$**, Fri & Sat, ***$w. Credit Cards**: None, Cash Only. **Bus Lines**: 206*, 301*.

Glass Pool Inn

4613 Las Vegas Boulevard South (800-527-7118, 739-6636) – One of the kinkier motels you'll find in this city, this alluring single story inn (maximum 48 rooms) has just what their name implies – a pool with glass windows. It was established in 1952, and judging by the faded marquee lettering, it hasn't changed too dramatically over the years. Still, the rooms are clean and the location (on the edge of the strip) is what makes this a very good bargain. **Location**: S. **Amenities:** Fresh linens, private bath, cable TV with HBO and a phone for local calls, pets are allowed, and a most stylish pool. **Credit Cards**: Visa, MasterCard, American Express and Discover. **Rates: $$,** Sun.-Thurs., **$$$**, Fri.-Sat., ***$w. Bus Lines:** 301*, 302*.

Motel 6

195 E. Tropicana Avenue at Koval Lane (800-466-8356, 798-0728), www.motel6.com – What kind of budget guide would this be if it didn't include a Motel 6? This long-standing chain of budget motels naturally has one in Vegas. If you've ever stayed in one, then you know what to expect: cleanliness, dependability and friendliness. The location, a ten to fifteen minute walk east of the strip, is what makes this a good value. **One Note of Caution:** You don't need a budget guide to know that Motel 6 is a very popular source of inexpensive lodging. That said, the vacancy here tends to be full. Call in advance to reserve a room for any season. **Location**: OS. **Amenities:** cable TV with HBO, a phone for free local calls, and pets are allowed. **Credit Cards**: Visa, MasterCard, American Express and Discover. **Rates: $$**, Sun.-Thurs., **$$$**, Fri.-Sat. **Bus Lines:** 201*, 301*, 302*.

Las Vegas Backpackers Hostel and Adventure Center

1322 Fremont Street at 13th Street (800-550-8958, 385-1150), www.hostels.com.us.nv.html – Highly regarded as the best place in town for the backpack set. It was recently renovated from an old Howard Johnson's and is now an attractive three-story hostel with plenty of familiar comforts for the hostel traveler. You have your choice of a bunk in a dorm room that holds up to five guests, or a single room with a private bath. Among the comforts: satellite TV, heated swimming pool/jacuzzi (24 hr. access), lounge area, a multilingual staff, pool tables, an open bar, access to the internet, and best of all, NO CURFEW – what more could you ask for? There's even a courtesy shuttle to take you to the heart of the strip. The only drawback – this hostel is located in an older and sometimes unsavory part of town. Like any major city with a low-income lodging area, avoid underlit areas at night and be cautious. You must have a student ID or youth hostel card to stay here. Reservations are strongly recommended in the summer. **Location:** DT. **Amenities:** Mentioned above. **Credit Cards:** Visa, MasterCard, American Express and Discover. **Dorm Bed: $** Daily **Private Room: $$** Daily, **Bus Lines:** 107*, 301*.

Las Vegas International Hostel

1208 Las Vegas Boulevard South at Oakey Boulevard (385-9955) – This is Las Vegas' other youth hostel. It's not as upscale as the backpacker's hostel. The carpeting is a little tattered, the walls need a paint job, and you don't get your own TV. The location, right on Las Vegas Boulevard, is its notable virtue. The dorms fit four to six people, and there are only six private rooms, so call in advance if you want to reserve one of these. Office hours are from 7-11am and 3-11pm. **Location:** DT. **Amenities:** You share a bath in the dorm, but you get your own in the private rooms. The furnishings are far from high quality, but it's rock bottom cheap. **Credit Cards:** none, only cash or traveler's checks. **Dorm Bed: $** nightly for both students and non-students, ***$w. Private Room: $$** nightly. **Bus Line:** 301*.

Chapter 3

Getting Hitched

Nothing rivals Las Vegas when it comes to exchanging wedding vows. This is the only city in the country where you can get married drive-though window style, or have the ceremony presided by an Elvis impersonator! The other advantage of getting married here is that it's very simple. No blood test or long waiting period is required, and the ceremonies are cheap. You can get a license at the **Clark County Marriage License Bureau, 200 S. 3rd St. and Bridger, (455-3156), Hours: Mon.–Thurs., 8am-Midnight, Fri-Sun., 8am-until midnight.** Both the licenses and the ceremony are just $35, cash only. Both parties must be eighteen, and you need at least two witnesses. If you don't have any witnesses handy, find someone loitering in a nearby casino, or better yet, *pay* someone you find loitering at a nearby casino. $10 will normally do the trick. If you're going to have it performed at a strip chapel, ask the chaplain performing the service if they have an employee they can spare. More often than not, they'll oblige. One last note of advice: tip the court appointee who performs the service. Hey, this is Vegas — it's a necessity!

To some of you it might seem silly to evaluate our "strip" chapels, as you would a record store or a restaurant. It's all a matter of personal taste. These chapels are strictly small, freestanding outlets. Many of the major strip hotels (Bally's, Tropicana, Treasure Island) have chapels that are dazzling in scope and imagination, but they can be e-x-p-e-n-s-i-v-e. It's best to stick with what I've listed here for a good value. What some of these chapels can create for you on a limited budget just might surprise you. Always remember that, although there is no "fee" for the minister's service, a "donation" for his services is strongly suggested and is normally around $40.

The most popular months for a wedding in this town are May and June; not coincidentally these are the nicest months of the year weather-wise. Planning to wed on Valentine's Day? Good luck to you — start making your calls *months* in advance.

For the non-traditionalists (i.e. same-sex couples) there are a few chapels in town that will do a "commitment" ceremony. Some of the chapels I called were insufferably self-righteous. "It's illegal" or "a minister can lose his license," was the occasional reply. Not true, according the County Clerk. These ceremonies are "symbolic" and therefore are approached without any legal entanglements, but strictly as a gesture of love. So while it won't be legal, at least the pomp and festivity is available for you. Chapels that offer these services are duly noted in the entries. All of these chapels accept major credit cards, so if you're in the mood for any additional services, it's all at your disposal. A limousine, hot-air balloon, and cliched sentiments like cupids, valentines, hearts, and the ever popular unity candle, can all be arranged, at a price of course – making that piece of plastic money all the more valuable.

The Candlelight Wedding Chapel

2855 Las Vegas Boulevard South near the Riviera Hotel (800-962-1818, 735-4179), www.candlelightchapel.com – One of the more popular strip chapels in the city. They'll make arrangements for you to wed in a hot-air balloon, in an underwater tank, and any other kind of bizarre backdrop you can think of, for a price of course. Packages run from $169-$499. **Bus Line:** 301*.

Divine Madness Fantasy Wedding Chapel

111 Las Vegas Boulevard South at Fremont Street (800-717-4734, 384-5660), www.fantasychapel.com – Now here's a wild and wicked place to have a wedding. Throw out all those traditional notions you had about ceremonies, because "Divine Madness" is truly just what the name implies. It's as if you stumbled upon a gloriously gaudy rummage sale at a North Hollywood apartment complex. You'll see a variety of outfits when you walk into the chapel, such as S&M leather, Wild West cowpoke, and gaudy Renaissance outfits complete with beaded headrests. Liberace would have loved this place! The packages run anywhere between $175- $275. Commitment Ceremony services are available. **Bus Line:** 301*.

San Francisco Sally's Victorian Wedding Chapel

1304 Las Vegas Boulevard South north of Oakey Boulevard (800-658-8677, 385-7777) – A small chapel that cannot seat more than 20 people, San Francisco Sally's still makes the grade by the sheer enthusiasm of its owners, Luanne Baker and Joy Seaman. Luanne and Joy lovingly dovetail your every step toward planning your wedding. The store is filled with traditional tuxes and gowns plus additional accessories like boutiques and candles. During the ceremony there's even the sound of a recorded harpist. This might sound a bit precious, but it's highly appropriate given the context of Victorian frills in this warm, quaint chapel. If you want to wed in a place complete with velvet chairs and old-styled silver tea sets, then Sally's is for you. Prices range from a basic ceremony ($95) to a full package ($370). Added bonus, Sally's is one of the few places that covers the minister's donation fee in their packages, so they inform you not to slip him or her two 20's. **Bus Line**: 301*.

Silver Bells Wedding Chapel

607 Las Vegas Boulevard South at Bonneville Avenue (800-221-8492, 382-3727), www.silverbell.com – A typical, Vegas, no-frills wedding chapel. The interior isn't the swankiest in town, in fact it's pretty threadbare, but the exterior is pleasant. There's even a small garden with a tiny bridge over a little creek – cute touch. A basic package will cost you just $60 and the semi-elaborate one around $190. Keep a watch for this chapel's employees. They'll be on the boulevard handing out coupons that can save you up to 20% off the pre-packaged price. The basic includes a witness, wedding music, and a marriage scroll. Hey, what did you expect for $60? **Bus Line:** 301*.

Cupid's Wedding Chapel

827 Las Vegas Boulevard South at Hoover Street (800-543-2933, 598-4444), www.cupidswedding.com – They're game for all kinds of ceremonies here: religious, civil, traditional Jewish, marriage renewals, Family Unity services and Lesbian & Gay commitments. Cupid's other attribute, besides their welcoming, open-minded attitude, is a pleasant low-frills chapel complete with pews, and a lovely stained glass backdrop filled with doves and roses. The basic service starts at $85 and more elaborate packages can go up to $500. **Bus Lines:** 206*, 301*.

A Little White Chapel

1301 Las Vegas Boulevard South north of Oakey Boulevard (800-545-8111, 382-5943), www.alittlewhitechapel.com – This celebrated chapel had the first drive-up window marriage ceremony in Las Vegas. Although their ingenious idea has been much imitated since, Little White is still tops in the drive-up category because of its quick efficiency. How quick? It's available 24 hours, will cost just $25, and you don't need to call ahead for an appointment – besides whoever heard of reservations at a drive-through window? The basic service starts at just $45 and is a true bargain. You'll get candlelight service, music, limousine, and a witness if you need one. Other packages include the $259/Regular (pictures, a corsage and boutonniere) and the $559/Joan Collins Special — yes she was married here once — (bridal bouquets, champagne, a wedding cake, plus much more). It's also the site of many celebrity weddings. Among the "stars" that have been hitched here include Michael Jordan, Judy Garland, Demi Moore and Bruce Willis, and Frank Sinatra. You don't believe me? Just take a peek in the lobby to see autographed photos of popular personalities plastered everywhere. The starting price for a basic wedding is $85. Commitment Ceremony services are available. **Bus Line:** 301*.

A Wee Kirk o' the Heather

231 Las Vegas Boulevard South at Bridger Avenue (800-843-5266, 382-9830), www.weekirk.com – The name is Scottish for "A Little Chapel of the Heather" (in the Scottish Highlands, the Heather is a flower that brings good luck). This is the oldest strip chapel in the city, dating all the way back to 1940, and it's captivating and simple. All the rooms are draped in virginal white (the striking white roses that adorn the stage is a nice touch), has excellent seating capacity, and, of course, a waiting room for the nervous parties involved. There's an easy grace to this place that makes this a definite look on your list for strip chapels. It's $49 for the basic service, but it's a bargain for just $30 more to get 12 professional photographs (you keep the negatives) or a complete recording of the wedding on video. This includes the use of their silk flower arrangements. Commitment Ceremony services are available. **Bus Line:** 301*.

A Special Memory Wedding Chapel

800 S. 4th Street at Gass Street (800-962-7798, 384-2211), www.aspecialmemory.com – The closest thing you'll find to a wedding-themed, indoor mini-mall. Florists, tuxedo rentals, a bridal shop and three wedding chapels are all available at your disposal. The décor is considerably more upscale than most. You can't help but notice the stained glass windows, the podium and seats which are carved from rich oak, burgundy carpeting, and a euphoric atmosphere of light tinsel and velvet that echoes the ambience of a Vincent Minnelli musical. If you want something in the no-frills department, this chapel also offers a drive-up window wedding for just $25 — and that is where the inexpensiveness of this place stops. Next on the price list are their "special memories" packages, which are a lot fancier, and therefore more expensive. Their *cheapest* service starts at $176 and includes complimentary limousine service, bride and groom carnation bouquet, and a professional photographer. Anything else beyond this and you'll pay around $300-$400. Commitment Ceremony services are available. **Bus Lines:** 207, 401.

Sweethearts Wedding Chapel

1155 Las Vegas Boulevard South at Charleston Boulevard (800-444-2932, 385-7785) — Clearly one of the more pleasant offerings in town for both civil and religious ceremonies. For just $65, you'll get a package that includes photos, videos and even a line of formal wear. If you want to spend a little more money, they've got the goods on the premises: music, witnesses, flowers, and even limousine service. **Hours:** 10am–10pm, daily. **Bus Line:** 301*.

Graceland Wedding Chapel

619 Las Vegas Boulevard South at Bonneville Avenue (800-824-5732, 474-6655), www.gracelandchapel.com

— A very lovely and unique wedding chapel that has been operating for over 50 years. The podium and seats are all white and there are gorgeous flowers adorning the walls. The prices start with a simple, no-frills ceremony with use of the chapel, witness and music for just $50 and prices go up from there. Flowers ($6), photographs ($40), or a professional videotape of the service ($50) are all for the asking. Many famous celebrities have been hitched here. Among them, Jon Bon Jovi and Lorenzo Lamas! Commitment Ceremony services are available. **Bus Line:** 301*.

Chapter 4

Shopping

Like any other major city that caters to tourists (i.e. New York, Chicago, Atlanta, etc.), Las Vegas really does offer something for everyone. All the essentials: clothes, books, records, and other neat gift ideas, can be found for an extremely low price. I hope this chapter helps you find something interesting that will serve your memories.

Records, CDs, Cassettes and Videos

For those who love musical diversity and digging around a metropolis for a rare record item, Las Vegas will surprise you with what it has to offer. In the last six years, Las Vegas has seen such an increase in its demographics (particularly among its youth) that it was only a matter of time that some excellent record stores sprang up around the city that could both tailor an idiosyncratic taste and not crimp one's budget. Here is an off-handed selection of some of the more frugal bargains and worthwhile shopping places that are not too far from the main thrust of the city, and they all accept major credit cards. I have even included the payment policy for the used record stores. If you find yourself short on money, you just might want to sacrifice some of the CDs you're slightly less partial to for some quick cash. Hey, I once worked at a used record store — this happened a lot.

New Records, CDs, Cassettes and Videos

Tower Records

4580 W. Sahara Avenue at Decatur Avenue (364-2500), www.towerrecords.com — This particular Tower Records merged with the **Good Guys**, a huge, sprawling multimedia store that has the latest goodies for techno freaks. It's pretty impressive for the sheer volume of merchandise they carry. CDs, cassettes, Videos, and DVDs are just some of the items you'll find here, and it can even yield some surprises if you're looking for that hard to find artist or tape. Sales include some cutout merchandise and previously listened to CDs in both stores. **Hours:** 10am-Midnight. **Bus Lines:** 103, 204.

Odyssey Records

1600 Las Vegas Boulevard South at Oakey Boulevard (384-4040) — This store has been around for a while, and believe it or not, you can spot a celebrity now and then. Andre Agassi and Brook Shields have been caught browsing in this store (during happier times), as have famed magicians and local residents Penn and Teller. As for the music, the selection has thinned out over the years, but Odyssey is still known for their excellent import and local/indie selection — particularly strong is the selection of Hip-Hop, Latino and Reggae in the used CD section, with prices starting at $6.95. Prices are a bit high for the newer stuff, but now and then a sale will come along. Its location on the boulevard makes it a convenient place to shop. **Hours**: 24 hours a day, seven days a week. **Bus Line:** 301*.

Virgin Megastore at Caesar's Forum Shops

3500 Las Vegas Boulevard South at Flamingo Road (696-7100) — This recent addition to the Forum Shops is just as impressive as the Virgin stores in New York or San Francisco. There's plenty of diversity to be found: jazz, rock, house, rap, R&B, third world, international, opera and well, you get the idea. The first floor is all music and the second floor is everything else (books, videos, computer software and a surprisingly inexpensive coffee shop). They also have a plethora of listening stations so you can get familiar with the latest music. Prices are a little high. After all, they are renting space from Caesar's Forum Shops, where dining at Spago and shuffling in Gucci shoes is the trend, yet true music lovers drool at the most comprehensive import selection in town, which suprisingly can be anywhere from $2-$4 cheaper than at Tower or Odyssey. **Hours**: 10am – Midnight. **Bus Lines:** 202*, 301*, 302*.

Used Records, CDs, Cassettes and Videos

J-Mar's Records

2620 S. Maryland Parkway at Sahara Avenue (796-6366) — A pop cultural heaven for those who want to dig through the bins for their old favorite 33s and 45s. It's all here: videos, CDs, old vinyls, laserdiscs and even some posters. The staff is knowledgeable and their selection and prices for used Jazz and Blues CDs are terrific. Although this shop is frequented by people of all ages, those with a more youth-oriented taste in music may not be too ebullient about the CD collection, which is limited to either classic rock (Zepplin, Stones, Beatles, Elton John) or contemporary heavy metal (Metallica, Queensryche). If you're looking for newer stuff with an alternative bent, you should go elsewhere. **Buy and Trade Policy** — pretty tight, since the owners are extremely picky about what they want on their shelves. Still, their prices are consistent — you'll get $4 for a CD, and videos and cassettes go for 50¢. Money for vinyls depends on condition and salability. Trades are equal to the buying price. **Hours:** 11am-6pm, daily. **Bus Lines:** 109*, 204

The Underground

1164 E. Twain Avenue at Maryland Parkway (733-7025) — Las Vegas's oldest used record store (est. 1980) is not nearly as busy as it once was, and sadly the recent swelling of larger used CD stores means the Underground isn't getting the customers like it had in the past to trade or sell merchandise. Despite their waning selection, you can still stumble upon some gems at the Underground for alternative and indie music. I recently bought the "Story of the Clash" two-CD set for only $11, when other stores were quoting $16-$20. I also purchased an import Undertones CD in mint condition for only $7 when other stores (like Record City) were quoting $15. Another big plus for this store is its information on many local bands in Las Vegas's alternative scene. Ads for latest gigs can be found on a bulletin board near the front of the store. The Underground also has a cool collection of posters, cassettes, books and other campy memorabilia. If you have any questions, direct them to Brent, the store manager, who will be happy to talk to you. **Buy and Trade Policy** — Pretty fair, with $3-$4 for a CD and just a little more for a truly rare item. Cassettes will fetch you 50¢. Trades are even to the buys. **Hours:** 11:30am-8pm, Mon-Sat., Noon-5pm, Sun. **Bus Lines:** 109*, 203, 213.

Big B's

4761 S. Maryland Parkway at University Road (732-4433) — Located a block south of UNLV, this store has some great bargains on CDs. Their selection of classic rock is outstanding (Cream, Blind Faith, Yardbirds, Queen and many more). Overstock items for some name acts like the Pretenders and the Kinks can be found for as little as $4.98! The average price for a CD is around $7.98. **Buy and Trade Policy** — A little cheap, you'll get anywhere from $1-$3 for CDs and the only vinyls they're interested in are collectibles. **Hours:** 11am-9pm, Mon-Sat, Noon-6pm, Sun. **Bus Lines:** 109*, 213.

Sound Barrier

4800 Maryland Parkway, Suite K at Tropicana Avenue (228-2763) – This is a pretty small record store located two blocks south of UNLV. The variety is terrific, with plenty of hard-to-find indie acts and strong support for local acts – but expect to pay top dollar. Used CDs are slightly better; with name acts (Nine Inch Nails, Chili Peppers, etc.) hovering around the $10 mark. Vintage LPs of classic punk acts from the '70s and '80s are also available. One of the best aspects of Sound Barrier is its support of local bands. Like the Underground, they have a bulletin board that advertises what's up with new acts in town. You can even find recruitment cards left by burgeoning bands that are searching for other musicians to flesh out their sound. **Buy and Trade Policy** – Marginal, you'll get anywhere from $2-3, possibly $4, for a *very* rare item or an import. The trades are equal to the buy. **Hours:** 11am-8pm, Mon-Sat, Noon-5pm, Sun. **Bus Line:** 109*.

The Wherehouse

4555 W. Charleston Boulevard at Essex Drive (259-6606), www.wherehouse.com – This national chain has become more appealing to the bargain hunter since it started selling used CDs in their stores. The Las Vegas branch has a selection that is varied and well organized. Used CD prices range from $4-$8. Best of all, there are several listening stations for you to check the sound quality of the CDs. **Buy and Trade Policy** – A little stiff, not surprising given the low prices. You'll get an average of $2-$4 per CD. They offer a trade special every Tuesday, five used CDs for a brand new one, but true bargain hunters should take the cash to purchase the cheaper, used stuff. **Hours:** 10am-10pm, except for Tue (10am-8pm) and Sat (10am-11pm). **Bus Lines:** 103, 206*.

Wax Trax Records

2909 S. Decatur Boulevard at Edna Street (362-4300) – The name Wax Trax Records says it all — a store primarily for collectors that deal with classic *vinyls*. The albums are all over the place (literally and metaphorically), with big band, blues, jazz, and contemporary hard rock. The 45s are also impressive, ranging from classic '50s doo-wop (the Platters), sharp '60s Brit invasion (the Kinks, the Who), cool '70s art rock (Roxy Music, David Bowie) to snazzy '80s new wave (the Go-Go's, Missing Persons – sadly, 45s dried up after this period). In terms of organization – well, just prepare yourself for a long chore because you'll have to *dig* since the inventory is jam packed in a two-story house. However, I need to warn you, these items *are not cheap.* Mama Cass dolls, Fonzie lunch pales, rare Beatles items, teen fanzines featuring Bobby Sherman on the cover, and in some cases, vintage 45s, can cost quite a bit. Yet, given the undying love and demand for nostalgia in the collectors market, it isn't too much out of step. Only the books, which are pretty ordinary in their variety and pop cultural value, aren't up to snuff. It's important to note that this store doesn't really encourage casual browsing. If you're not recognized as a regular, you're often asked up front by the owners what it is you're looking for and if you don't have a definite idea, the red carpet doesn't exactly come rolling out. Still, if you're curious to find that rare, odd record for your collection, it is worth the stop. **Hours**: 10am-5pm, Mon-Sat, closed Sun. **Bus Line**: 103.

Books

There is no point in comparing the literati of Las Vegas to say, New York or San Francisco. Subsequently, the booksellers market isn't as strong as those cities, especially for out-of-print books or collectibles. Still, Las Vegas has come a long way in the last few years with numerous new and used bookstores that have opened up all over the valley. It takes a some diligence, but you can find almost anything you want.

New Books

Barnes & Nobles

2191 N. Rainbow Boulevard at Lake Mead Boulevard (631-1775) and 3860 S. Maryland Parkway at Twain Avenue (734-2900), www.bn.com – Say what you will about this chain, but this big and easygoing bookstore is justly popular because you can read for hours on a comfortable sofa and not fear anyone bothering you. The Rainbow branch has some particularly good discounts at the front of the store. **Hours:** 9am-11pm, daily. **Bus Lines:** Rainbow - 101, 210, 211; Maryland – 109, 213.

Bell, Book and Candle

1725 E. Charleston Boulevard at Bruce Street (386-2950) – Talismans, magic charms, fast-money potions for quick casino kills, quartz crystals and other witchcraft supplies can be found in this fascinating store. The eerily enticing atmosphere and the sly demeanor of the employees only accentuates the fun. A bit pricey, and I haven't a clue to what some of the inventory is about, but it's certainly worth the stop if only to browse. **Hours:** 11am-7pm, daily. **Bus Line:** 206*.

Bookstar

4630 Faircenter Parkway at Decatur Boulevard (877-1872) – Since the opening of both Barnes and Nobles and Borders in the last few years, this doesn't seem like the megastore it was once perceived to be. Still, they have some terrific deals. Their bargain selection, unlike other bookstores (which tend to carry damaged goods, old editions of dictionaries, and generally boring filler in its discount bin) is quite lively, ranging from classic literature to gorgeously illustrated coffee table books. **Hours:** 9am-10pm, daily. **Bus Lines:** 103, 206*.

Borders Bookshop

2323 S. Decatur Boulevard at Sahara Avenue (258-0999), 2190 N. Rainbow Boulevard at Lake Mead Boulevard (638-7866), www.borders.com – A huge, sprawling bookstore with arguably the best selection of books in town. If you are like most people I know, this store is a great timekiller between activities and appointments. Borders also has a lot of booksigning parties and musical acts, so call their event hotline **(258-6479)** for the latest information. The hip, low-key staff will seldom give you slack if you take some magazines or books to the cafe, so the option of enjoying a good read while drinking cappuccino or eating cake is a certainly appealing – just don't spill anything on the merchandise! **Hours:** Both branches – 9am-11pm. **Bus Lines:** Decatur – 103, 204, Rainbow – 101, 210, 211.

Gambler's Book Club

630 S. 11th Street at Charleston Boulevard (800-522-1777, 382-7555), www.gamblersbook.com – Even if you don't gamble, this is an amazing bookshop where you can browse for hours. It's the oldest bookstore of its kind in our city. Established in 1964, it offers books on every aspect of gaming, not just the casino variety. Casino games like baccarat and craps, general games like gin rummy and cribbage, sports betting books for racetracks, as well as organized professional sports are all available here. The level of scholarship and research detail that goes into these books that offer tips on how to gamble to your advantage is amazing. There are also video tapes and computer software to better your performance at the table. The customers who roam this store can be an eclectic bunch: from the Runyonesque gambler, complete with a fedora hat and a pick in his teeth, to a minister I once saw buying a book on how to throw the perfect bingo party for his church social. This in itself makes for fun observation. Be sure to check out their website, which offers a *complete* inventory of their store. **Hours:** 9am-5pm, Mon-Sat, closed Sun. **Bus Lines:** 109*, 206*.

Gamblers General Store

800 S. Main Street north of Charleston Boulevard (382-9903), www.ggss.com – If the Gamblers Book Club has the most thorough and impressive collection of gambling books, than this place is its companion for having the most thorough and impressive gaming hardware. Poker chips, cards, roulette wheels and slot machines are all available. While some of the items are a bit heavy for your carry-on bag on the plane, don't worry, they will ship. **Hours:** 9am-5pm, daily. **Bus Lines:** 105, 206*.

Great Wall Bookstore

4255 Spring Mountain Road, #C-105 in Chinatown Plaza (876-8875) – A very unique store, especially for those from a strictly western cultural persuasion. Magazines, calendars, books, CDs (classical Asian chamber music as well as very bad, if engaging, Japanese pop music – remember Pink Lady?) and most things normally associated with bookstores are here, just in another language. Please be patient with the Chinese merchants who act as the sales representatives. There might be a case of cultural misunderstanding since their straightforward demeanor can be off-putting to westerners, but don't let your apprehensions get in the way, these merchants really do want your business. **Hours:** 10am-9pm, daily. **Bus Line:** 203.

Tower Books

4580 W. Sahara Avenue at Arville Road (364-2500) – The books at Tower are geared more toward the pop market. They have a broad range of trash chick (youth culture, travel guides, music bio's, Betty Page calendars), a stellar collection of magazines from all over the world, and a good selection of fiction and nonfiction (historical, self-help, sociological, etc.). The store is spacious, and the subdued staff that will seldom pester you. **Hours:** 10am-Midnight. **Bus Line:** 204.

Used Books

Albion Book Co.

2466-G E. Desert Inn Road at Eastern Avenue (792-9554) — Las Vegas's largest used bookstore is justly popular with our city's more literate population, because it has something for almost every taste. Rarities, mysteries, fiction, non-fiction and sheet music are only the beginning in this 6,000-sq. ft. store. They can also mail order for you, just in case you'll be in town for a while. **Hours:** 10am-6pm., daily. **Bus Lines:** 110, 112

Book Magician

202 W. Charleston Boulevard, #2 at Rancho Road (384-5838) — A small bookstore, but not without its charm. You'll find very few collectibles or first editions, but you will find a variety of softbacks, various coffee table books and an especially strong collection of the paranormal. The prices are fairly reasonable. **Hours:** 9am-10pm, Mon-Sat. 11am-7pm, Sun. **Bus Lines:** 106, 206*

Bookends

3920-A W. Charleston Boulevard at Valley View Boulevard (878-9290) — Another store that has a Paranormal and Science Fiction bent. There's also an abundance of mystery and crime novels. Prices are reasonable (with the gross exception being the audio books, which are as little as a scant 10% off retail price). The location is fairly easy to get to from the main thrust of the city. **Hours:** 10am-6pm, Mon-Sat, closed on Sun. **Bus Lines:** 104, 206*.

Dead Poet Books

3874 W. Sahara Avenue at Valley View Boulevard (227-4070) – The usual stock of hardback and paperbacks, with an interesting emphasis on the military and the old west. They offer some good values and the managers are very polite and helpful. **Hours:** 10am-6pm, Mon-Sat. Noon-5pm, Sun. **Bus Lines:** 104, 204.

Comics and Memorabilia

Alternate Reality Comics

4800 S. Maryland Parkway, Suite D north of Tropicana Avenue (736-3673) – The best comic book store on the eastside of town. The owner, Ralph Mathieu, has done a tremendous job packing in all sorts of goodies. Posters, T-shirts and related supplies are all over the wall and ceiling. There's even a selection of cool Japanamation videos. The prices are moderate, but sometimes a great deal will come along. The last time I was in here, all back issues were 50% off! I bought some classic DC comics that were at least 15 years old for less than $10. **Hours:** 11am-7pm, Mon-Sat, Noon-6pm, Sun. **Bus Line:** 109*.

Cosmic Comics

3330 E. Tropicana Avenue at Eastern Avenue (451-6611) – This comic book store doesn't lag too far behind Alternate as the 2nd best comic book store in town. What it lacks in diversity in makes up for with very good deals. The owners, a pair of friendly, Harley-riding brothers named John and

David, are the friendliest, most informative pair of blokes I've ever met. They will go out of their way to help you find and order what it is you're looking for. If you join their Cosmic Club, you'll get 20% off all comic books, including sales. Anything in the Bronze Age (1971-Present) will get you 75% off if you're in this club. There are many sales up to 50% off on popular comics (like D.C. and Marvel), some with adult content (including the marvelous Harry Crumb or Lloyd Llewelyn) and some comics based on old television shows (Gomer Pyle, The Three Stooges, My Three Sons). So if you have even a *passing* interest in comics, this is your place. Cosmic also has storage boards and vinyl containers to help you preserve your merchandise. **Hours:** 11am-7pm, daily. **Bus Lines:** 110, 201*.

Dreamwell Comics

5706 W. Charleston Boulevard at Upland Street (870-1268) – This is one of Las Vegas's oldest comic book stores. It's a fun place that, despite running a little high on the collectibles (baseball cards, classic toys, matchbox cars etc.), has an impressive collection with its array of comics, back issues and comic supplies. Dreamwell deals with more comic paraphernalia than other comic bookstores, so it's not surprising that they're a little pickier about what they buy (i.e., it better be vintage and specific) for their collector's market. **Hours:** 10am-6pm, Mon-Sat, 10am-5pm, Sun. **Bus Lines:** 102, 206*.

Kool Kollectibles

5197 W. Charleston Boulevard at Brush Street (877-5665) and 953 E. Sahara Avenue in Commercial Center – Both stores offer an excellent selection of Japanamation comics, (Soleil Moon, Akiru, etc.) as well as those old stand-by DC's comics (Superman, Batman, etc.). Kollectibles also has a knockout collection of sports memorabilia. Baseball, basketball, and hockey are available in all kinds of forms: cards, T-shirts, and celebrity fanzines just to name a few. Prices are reasonable, but they seldom have sales. **Hours:** Both Branches — 10am-8pm, Mon-Sat, 11am-8pm, Sun. **Bus Lines:** Charleston — 103, 206*, Sahara — 109*, 204.

Clothing, Retro Clothing, Thrift Stores and the Rest

Las Vegas has improved greatly with its collection of alternative shopping venues. We have used clothing stores, psychic periphenalia and other shops that sell merchandise with a distinct difference that will no doubt tap your curiosity.

Retro clothing stores tend to cost a bit more, but they're a useful stop if only to observe the history of popular clothing in the last forty years. Another benefit is that these stores will sometimes pay a fairly decent price if you care to sell those old threads you stumble upon in your attic during spring cleaning. The buy and trade policies for them are not set in stone, and there's occasional room to haggle.

Thrift stores get their inventory from donations, so the selection isn't as varied — making for harder work to find something you want, but with diligence, you'll find some practical and even attractive clothing for next to nothing.

The "rest" is pretty self-explanatory. They are outlets that simply don't quite fit into a category of their own, but still make for some interesting buys.

The list of stores I've put together are among the most unique and accessible in town. All the stores listed below take major credit cards.

Buffalo Exchange

4110 S. Maryland Parkway at Flamingo Road (791-3960) — "Where recycling is always in style" has long been the motto for this popular store which, since opening its first branch in 1974 in Tempe, AZ, has been one of the leading purveyors of the recycled fashion craze on the west coast. It's certainly the most popular store of this type in Las Vegas and for good reason — they offer great stuff at low prices. If you've been to the other franchises in California or Arizona, you know what to expect: irresistible one-of-a-kind items like capri pants, leopard print scarves, cardigans, and pink stiletto heels that just scream from the Martin Denny, lounge-act era of the sixties. Men can have their choice of vintage clothing like cabana style shirts, Hawaiian bermudas, pork pie hats, and those ever-popular khakis. Check out their one-dollar, mark down items at the front register. I once found a narrow, '60s-like tie with a hand-drawn picture of John Lennon! The staff is trendy, but never too obtuse. If you're here in March or April, be sure to check out their Spring sidewalk sale. You can find items from mini-skirts to bowling sneakers for as little as $3. So popular is this store that rumor has it David Cassidy was seen buying a shirt and pants that he later wore for the 1997 Billboard Music Awards. Whether he has admitted to this, no one is exactly sure. **Hours:** 11am-7pm, Mon-Sat, Noon-8pm, Sun. **Buy and Trade Policy** — Cash, 35% of their reselling price, trade credit 40% of the reselling price. **Bus Lines:** 109*, 202*, 213.

The Attic

1018 S. Main Street at Charleston Avenue (388-4088), www.atticvintage.com – A very aggressive fashion outlet that specializes in vintage clothing. You've probably seen The Attic's colorful, national ads for Visa on television and you're also probably aware that they've pulled out all the stops in the décor. Broken mannequins are strewn everywhere, lunch pails lace the wall, used 45s are pressed on the floor, used bowling bags adorn the sides of the room, and loads of old appliances (TV's, blenders, radios etc.) just litter this place and evokes that feeling of off-the-cuff nostalgia. It also shows how aggressive this store is in attracting the ultra-hip clientele. Housed in a big, two-story building, you're sure to discover some of the coolest retro fashions. If you need any of the following: Phillipino golf sweaters, old army jackets, uniforms from old Las Vegas's businesses and hotels that have since closed, plastic go-go boots popularized by Twiggy and Judy Geeson in the era of late 1960s Swinging London, then you've found yourself a home. It's a little costly, and there is a $1 fee to purchase an entrance pass (the value is that it lasts a lifetime), but the fact that it's all consolidated under one roof makes shopping here very tempting, so bring your credit card. **Hours:** 9am-5pm, Mon-Sat, daily. **Buy and Trade**

Policy — Not nearly as generous as the Buffalo Exchange. Although they won't tell you outright what they'll pay, I've calculated around 10%-15% on the buys and only a scant more on the trades. Still, the buyer for this store can be flexible if you have some unique material. **Bus Lines:** 108, 206*.

Mastroianni Fashions

3900 Paradise Road south of Twain Avenue (369-1040), 1701 S. Decatur Boulevard at Oakey Boulevard (220-8567) – Looking for cheap, upscale apparel? This store has it: shoes, blazers, sportscoats, designer shirts, and slacks — some of which are imported from Europe and sold at Mastrionni for a tremendously low cost. Brand names like Carlo Morandi, Pierre Cardin, and Giorgio Brutini are on sale in all styles, sizes, fabrics and colors. I once bought a pair of Stacy Adams ostrich shoes that were retailed in the shopping mall for $229 and paid only $49, and they were *not* factory damaged. Discounts ranging from 25%-80% off market retail make this store a worthy stop, gentlemen, if you have the time and money. **Hours:** Both Stores – 10am-7pm, Mon-Sat, 11am-5pm, Sun. **Bus Lines:** Paradise – 108, Decatur – 103, 205.

Catholic Charities Thrift Store

808 S. Main Street at Bonneville Avenue (382-4604), 1767 N. Rancho Drive south of Vegas Drive (646-2150), see phone book for more listings – Catholic Charities' Thrift stores have some wicked fashions at ridiculously low prices. I once bought a silk vest for $3, a brown derby hat — the kind James Cagney wore in all those Warner Brother's gangster flicks — for $2, a couple of bow ties for 99¢ a piece, and some assorted dress shoes in acceptable condition for just $5. The best store among the branches is located on Main Street, a main artery for antique hunting in the downtown area. **Hours:** Both Stores – 10am-6pm, daily. **Bus Lines:** Main Street – 108, Rancho – 106, 209, Vegas Drive – 103, 209.

Goodwill of Southern Nevada

3011 N. Rainbow Boulevard at Cheyenne Avenue (656-1266), 4632 S. Maryland Parkway at Harmon Avenue (895-9917), see phone book for more listings – Goodwill sometimes has a reputation for distinctive threads, even by second-hand clothing standards, but the stores listed above will challenge those notions. The Rainbow store clearly has the best selection of used clothes (blouses, slacks, jackets). The Maryland store stands out for quaintly eccentric finds: clocks, strange paintings (when was the last time you saw a nylon-strung caricature of Elvis on a black velvet canvas?) and erotic board games (if you're lucky to find them that is, they never seem to stay on the shelf too long). **Hours:** Rainbow & Maryland – 9am-7pm, Mon-Thurs, 9am-9pm, Fri-Sat, 10am-6pm, Sun. **Bus Lines:** Rainbow – 101, 218, Maryland – 109*.

Caribbean Life Style

1151 Las Vegas Boulevard South at Charleston Boulevard (386-7022) – One of the hipper, more freewheeling places in the city. Walk right in and you'll hear old-time reggae blasting through at the store. Caribbean Life Style has got some great vintage records, of both reggae and ska. I'm not talking about Marley, Tosh, or Cliff (though they do have them) but some classic stuff like Desmond Dekker, Prince Buster, and even Millie Small. Cute T-shirts of the Donald Dreaduck and "How Can I Be A Rude Without Me Hat?" variety abounds — cool posters too. The store is run by Stan the Man, KUNV's (91.5 FM) DJ for the Reggae Hour every Sunday night at 5 pm. He is also one aggressive salesman, but man, he's a trip. Prices are average, but a sale does pop up on occasion. **Hours:** 10am-6pm, daily. **Bus Lines:** 206*, 301*, 302*.

Shoe Sizes Outlet

1370 E. Flamingo Road at Maryland Parkway (734-0000) – "The World's Largest Selection of Hard To Find Shoes!" state their ads. Incredibly, they're close to the mark with this claim. Among the variety of shoes available: dress, casual, walking, sandals, comfort, athletic and even clogs. They have over 10,000 pair in stock and in all sizes. It's pretty close to the strip, just a 10-minute drive heading east. **Hours:** 10am-6pm, Mon-Sat, Noon-4pm, Sun. **Bus Lines:** 109*, 202*.

Images of the East Gift Shop

4255 W. Spring Mountain Road, #C-102 at Arville Road in Chinatown Plaza (368-4010) — This is yet another cool store located in the Chinatown Mall. The bigger items are a bit expensive and heavy (do you really see yourself lugging a 60 lb. screen with a jade studded image of Buddha onto a plane?). However, some neat, small, and inexpensive items can be purchased. Small figurines of Confucius, some intriguing wind chimes with symbols representing Chinese astrology, and unique booklets of Buddhist prophecies are all less than $10. **Hours:** 10am-9pm, daily. **Bus Line:** 203.

Cinema Collectors

2238 Paradise Road at Sahara Avenue (369-6916) – An excellent place for some great movie memorabilia that's very reasonably priced. Lobby cards, posters, magnets, and old copies of film fanzines are all available. It's pointless to give you a price range since most vintage movie articles depend on age, condition and popularity of the issue or item. Still, I once bought an old issue of TV guide with Jack Paar on the cover dating back to 1958, and an old Bowery Boys lobby card from 1946, and they both cost only $5. There's a terrific staff who are extremely helpful in looking up the hardest to find titles, sharing your enthusiasm for the material and thus, making shopping here all the more fun. **Hours:** 11am-6pm, Mon-Sat. **Bus Lines:** 108, 204, 301*, 302* (just one block east of the strip).

Oriental Furniture and Futons

2167 N. Decatur Boulevard north of Lake Mead Boulevard (646-1818) – A great stop to buy some discounted import items. You'll find everything from Chinese astrology calendars, Japanese tea sets, jade jewelry, silk purses, vases, books on Confucianism, theatrical masks, honey soap, mah jah game sets, and pearl cream and the list goes on and on. You name it, they got it, and at reasonable prices to boot. Some of the products are literally 50% off retail value. Stop by, this place is a must for bargain shoppers. **Hours:** 10am-5pm, Mon-Sat, Noon-4pm, Sun. **Bus Lines:** 103, 210.

The Corner House Antiques

1655 E. Charleston Boulevard at 17th Street (387-0334) – A small antique store that specializes in film memorabilia. Movie stills, old fanzines, outtake strips from classic Hollywood films, and autographed photos of classic stars like Betty Grable and James Stewart makes for a fun romp, and all the aforementioned items are under $12. **Hours:** 10am–6pm, daily. **Bus Lines:** 206*.

Field of Dreams

1647 E. Charleston Boulevard at 17th Street (385-2770) – This antique store benefits from a very friendly staff and some neat pocket items. Pieces like old tintype pictures ($2), vintage corporate products like a 70-year old Pepsi bottle ($15), and a cool variety of old liquor flasks ($18), are just a few of many knickknacks carefully laid out in the store. **Hours:** 10am–6pm, daily. **Bus Line:** 206*.

Josette's

1632 E. Charleston Boulevard at 17th Street (641-3892) – This antique store has a great variety of stuff, particularly it's Native American crafts like baskets and pottery. Elsewhere, a fine collection of jewelry, glassware, eyeglass frames and pens are neatly aligned in an automated turnstile machine so you can browse uninterrupted. **Hours:** 11am–7pm, Mon-Sat, 11am–4pm, Sun. **Bus Line:** 206*.

The Exotic Pet Store

2105 N. Decatur Boulevard at Lake Mead Drive (631-7387) – The city's largest selection of reptiles, amphibians and other exotic pets. This store is filled with spiders, turtles, iguanas, snakes and all kinds of birds that require pretty low maintenance. The owner told me it costs only $10 a month to provide for a 2-foot garden snake. You can purchase a variety of books, food supplies and cages to help you in your upkeep of your unusual new pet. It's not as dangerous as it sounds — the sign on their store window offers "100% health guaranteed". It's a must for those of you with even the slightest taste for the bizarre. **Hours:** 10am-7pm, Mon-Sat, Noon-5pm, Sun. **Bus Line:** 103.

Opportunity Village Thrift Store

921 S. Main Street south of Bonneville Avenue (383-1082) – Very well-organized, with broad compartment sections for clothes, appliances, old records, and pottery, just to name a few. The old records can be a pleasant surprise, offering old 33s and 45s for just a dollar. The best section by far is the clothing. They have a neat collection of off-kilter stuff. Over the years I've found African afghan ceremonial robewear, navy uniforms, peddle pushers, beehive wigs, and those hip '60s golf sweater-shirts, (the kind Roland Gift wore on all those Fine Young Cannibals' videos) — all for under $10. It's worth noting that other vintage clothing stores will pay headhunters to ravage this place for their own stores, and then jack up the price by at least 300%! I've seen it *so* many times. Personally, I'd like to do the hunting myself and not pay the finder's fee. If you do too, stop in here. **Hours:** 9am-5pm, Mon-Sat, 10am-5pm, Sun. **Bus Lines:** 108, 205.

Little Baja

3360 S. Decatur Boulevard at Desert Inn Road (873-5556) – This is a fascinating place featuring handcrafted Mexican Art. While it might seem intimidating at first when you approach their shop (a 20 ft. Aztec fountain, or a 30 ft. garden statue will greet you right off the street), kettles, hand-embroidered blankets, glass-blown balls, ceramic mugs, and bronze ashtrays are just some of the unique items that can be purchased for under $15. The informative staff will go out of their way to define just what it is you're looking at, so feel free to ask questions if you're not familiar with Aztec culture. **Hours:** 9am-5pm, Mon-Sat, 10am-3pm, Sun. **Bus Line:** 103.

Bonanza – The World's Largest Gift Shop

2460 Las Vegas Boulevard South at Sahara Avenue (385-7359) – The world's largest gift shop? Perhaps it had a run for the title when this beloved, tacky, "Vegas Memorabilia" store opened in 1972, but that's not the case now. Still, this is one of the best, widely stocked, and relatively inexpensive souvenir shops you'll find in town. This is the store all the locals recommend to their friends and relatives when they want to grab a piece of Vegas before they go home – Elvis lighters, dice soap on a rope, and my favorite – doggie biscuits in the shape of poker chips. Hey, kitsch obsession doesn't get any more buoyant than this! **Hours:** 8am–Midnight, daily. **Bus Lines:** 204, 301*, 302*.

The Psychic Eye

6848 W. Charleston Boulevard at Rainbow Boulevard (255-4477), 4810 Spring Mountain Road at Decatur Boulevard (368-7785) – If it's the paranormal you're interested in, then by all means give this place a try. Psychic arts, candle magic, books on meditation, tarot card readings, astrology charts, oils and aromatherapy are just part of this store's inventory. The atmosphere in these stores is very dark — velvet curtains are draped everywhere, blocking out most of the sunlight, and your nostrils will be filled with the obligatory Asian incense sticks (which are rapidly becoming a cliché in signifying herbal sophistication). Nevertheless, the Psychic Eye is a fascinating stop since it completely immerses itself in these intriguing, new age offerings. **Hours**: Both Branches – 10am-9pm, Mon-Fri, 10am-8:30pm, Sat, 11am-6pm, Sun. **Bus Lines:** Charleston – 101, 206*, Spring Mountain – 103, 203.

The Clay Shop

5755 Spring Mountain Road east of Jones Boulevard (871-9116) – There are some neat gift ideas in this store that has a wide selection of handcrafted pottery. Their showroom is fun, even if it would take a flatbed to lift some of the more heavy items. The more moderately priced and portable items include pots, vases, mirror frames, and — be sure to check this one out — a coconut bark basket. **Hours:** 10am-6pm, Mon.-Sat., 11am-5pm, Sun. **Bus Lines:** 103, walk two blocks west, 203.

Lost Vegas Gift Shop

101 E. Charleston Boulevard at Main Street, 2nd Floor in the Arts Factory (388-8857) – Every oddity ever related to Vegas culture is represented in this appealing little gift shop located on the second floor of the Arts Factory. You'll find Area 51 "x-ray" goggles ($4), lunch pails adorned with images of the "Rat Pack" ($8), Elvis coffee mugs ($3), giant bug back-scratchers (no doubt influenced by all those insect fear films of the cold war) ($6), as well as many t-shirts, maps and other gifts of related ilk. **Hours:** Noon-4pm, Tue-Sat. **Bus Lines:** 105, 206*.

Mr. Bill's Pipe and Tobacco Company

4632 S. Maryland Parkway at Delmar Street (739-8840), 4441 W. Flamingo Road at Arville Road (221-9771), see website for full listings, www.mr-bills.com – The most popular pipe and tobacco store in the city. An excellent value both for their variety and prices. There are several locations for this franchise, but these two are the biggest and most centrally located. Pipes, tobaccos, cigars, pouches, and a cool selection of tin boxes are all in stock. Best of all are their prices. There is always a special of some kind in all locations, whether it's a carton of Cloves (15%) off, Macanudo and Partagas cigars (20%) off, or Zippo and Colibri lighters (30%) off. The variety of stuff and discounts puts their competitors to shame. **Hours:** All Branches - 10am-9pm, Mon-Sat, 10am-8pm, Sun. **Bus Lines:** Maryland – 109*, Charleston – 206*.

Diversity

2310 S. Las Vegas Boulevard (382-8820) south of Oakey Boulevard, 4700 S. Maryland Parkway across UNLV (736-0916), see phone book for more listings – Freethinking customers from all over the city come here in droves, thanks to the store's strong diversity (hence the name) of products and services: tattoos, body piercing (the cheapest in town – only $20), jewelry, pipes, "herbal ecstasies," graffiti, T-shirts, and anything else of this milieu. There are at least a dozen or so tattoo artists who are well respected for their artistry, relative speed, and clean work. All walk-ins are welcomed. The UNLV branch offers tube (glass) blowing of over 420 shapes, varieties and colors in any design you want – made to order! As for customer service, the Las Vegas Boulevard store, perhaps because of the more diverse selection of tourists they must deal with, is a little more consumer-oriented than the University branch. This eccentric place is really an eyeful, so it's a must to see in this city. **Hours:** Both Branches – 10am-10pm, daily **Bus Lines:** Strip – 301*, Maryland – 109*, 201*.

Chapter 5

Food

If you've ever been to Las Vegas before, it didn't take you long to discover, with advertisements all over town and in local publications, that this city has no shortage of culinary fare. Most casinos love advertising cheap buffets and graveyard specials to bring you in the door, wisely knowing that a majority of you will hit the slots. While there's no denying that such feasts can meet anyone's desire for gluttony head on, you'll eventually get tired of the brass and noise of the casinos and seek something with a little more style. There are many varied and interesting places to eat in the city, so why not check them out? I've listed close to a hundred restaurants, delis, bakeries and other eateries in town, as well as some of the better specials on the strip, so I can't imagine you won't find something you like. A few of these restaurants accept cash only, or a minimum purchase for use of a credit card. As for the price range listed, keep in mind that it's a reflection of the average price of an entree. A restaurant might have a specialty dish or two that exceeds the scale, but that's generally the exception.

Restaurants and Eateries

The restaurants listed here are both free-standing establishments and those that are affiliated with casinos. My criteria was simple for those I wanted to recommend for this book: quality, portions, prices (entrees mostly $15 or less), service, and atmosphere — and not necessarily in this order, because some establishments have certain strengths over others. On the whole, these are places I would go back to for a second visit.

The scale breakdown is as follows:
$ Under $5 $$ Between $5-$10 $$$ Over $10

Asian & Pacific Islands

Aloha Specialty's

12 Ogden Avenue, 2nd Floor in the California Hotel (382-0338) — The late Sam Boyd, who originally owned the California Hotel, retired in Hawaii and hit upon the ingenious idea of arranging cheap airfare and lodging for the people of his newfound home. Ever since, Hawaiians have been faithfully staying at the California Hotel and the result is an atmosphere that locals call "little Honolulu". All the food and gift shops here offer quality stuff, but it's Aloha Specialty's that has all the natives talking. You can get a big bowl of Saimin (buckwheat noodles) with BBQ beef, a hot plate of Chicken Katsu (cutlet), or Chicken Teriyaki with veggies for less than $5! If you feel like grabbing something more elaborate, try their stomach-stretching dinners. The Kalua Pig with Cabbage is popular, as is their Sweet and Sour Spare Ribs with Pork Tofu. All dinners come with a side of rice and macaroni salad (a must in the Hawaiian diet). Side dishes like Spam Masubi, and Kim Chee are also available. Beware of Friday and Saturday nights, the food here is so good you could wait in line for as long as 40 minutes. Credit Cards are not accepted. **Hours:** 9am-10:30pm, Mon-Thurs, 9am-11pm, Fri-Sat, 9am-9pm, Sun. **Price Range:** $-$$, **Bus Lines:** 106, 108, 205.

Classic Buffet House

3331 E. Tropicana Avenue at Pecos Road (435-2226) – It's basically an all-you-can-eat Chinese and Japanese Buffet and they serve everything you'd expect for these two cultural food groups, including Sweet and Sour Chicken, Moo Goo Gai Pan, and Chicken or Beef Teriyaki. Lunchtime during the weekdays is usually pretty crowded, and service can get a little slow. The simple, elegant décor (everything is done in saturated off-white, from the walls to the table) makes it quite attractive. If you want gluttony, you've got it here. Lunch is $6.95, Dinner is $8.95, but drinks are *not* included. **Hours:** 11-9 pm, Mon-Fri., 11-9:30 pm Sat & Sun. **Price Range:** $$, **Bus Lines:** 111, 201*.

Dragon Sushi

4115 Spring Mountain Road, #101 (368-4336) – A terrific, casual and inexpensive place for some good Japanese food. It's a bit on the small side (it doesn't hold more than a maximum of 49 people), yet people crowd in here during lunchtime because they have some very good specials. I recommend the Chicken Teriyaki with salad or the California Roll lunch special (although you die-hards may not consider the California Roll traditional sushi, it's still tasty) for $4.95. The dinners are a good bargain too. Try their combination plates: Beef or Chicken Teriyaki with lightly battered tempura, complete with salad, fruit and soup. If that's too much, try their Rice and Noodle, Chicken Tendon, Tempura or Nabeyaki Udon and savor it as the piping hot steam from the broth opens up your nasal passages. The sushi counter holds about 15 people. The prices per roll are pretty fair: two pieces of the Red Clam, Yellow Tail, Salmon, or Scallop are just $4. The décor is quaintly elegant. The walls and tables are colored in soft greens, there are uniquely designed mirrors all around (a laughing Buddah on one), and pictures of rickshaws and other emblems of Japanese culture abound, but it's all arranged in a way that's never intrusive to your dining space. Finally soft, traditional Japanese music plays in the background. Add it all up, and you have a soothing, pleasant dining experience. **Hours:** 11:30-10:30 pm, Daily. **Price Range:** $$-$$$, **Bus Line:** 203.

Makino

3965 S. Decatur Boulevard, #5 at Flamingo Road (889-4477) – Las Vegas' best all-you-can-eat sushi deal. There are over 40 kinds of glorious sushi spread over a 160 ft. table.

Among the highlights for the lunch buffet ($12.95, $13.95 on weekends, 11am–2:30pm): scallop, octopus, nago, tuna, clam, red snapper, and for you non-traditionalists, the California and Philly rolls. You can try the salad bar, fried rice, noodle soup, sweet and sour chicken or shrimp and vegetable tempura. The dinner buffet ($21.95, $22.95 on weekends, 5am–11pm) is more expensive, but you'll get all of the above plus jumbo shrimp, fresh oysters, snow crab legs, and sashimi. The service is excellent — your hot tea or other beverages will rarely be allowed to run low. The wine selection isn't great (Zifandel, Chardonnay and White Plum) and at $4.50 a glass not exactly a bargain, but the food makes up for that. The only disappointment is with the desserts. Little bite-sized cookies, a small cup of chocolate mousse and fruit gelatin won't have you running to the dessert tray with gleeful abandon, but you'll be so stuffed with the sushi that I'll doubt this will be a problem for you. **Hours**: Lunch – 11:30am-2:30pm, Mon-Thurs, 11:30am-3pm, Fri-Sun; Dinner – 5:30pm-9pm, Mon-Thurs, 5:30pm-10pm, Fri-Sun. **Price Range**: $$$ **Bus Line**: 103, 202*.

Edo of Japan

4300 Meadows Lane, 2nd Floor in the Meadows Mall (878-5353) — When we think of food courts at suburban shopping malls, we think of banality and/or high prices. Surprisingly, Edo of Japan is neither. If you happen to be at the Meadows Mall, be sure to have lunch here. The variety isn't much, but the Grilled Chicken Teriyaki Salad, Teriyaki Chicken Bowl, Beef Sukiyaki, and Ginger Chicken are all tasty and healthier than the usual mall food court fare like deep-fried cheese on a stick, or a cinnabon. Plus, the prices are hard to beat – all of the above mentioned dishes are under $5! What's the drawback? This is a mall with an open-air food court, and is sometimes packed with very talkative teenagers, so a quiet lunch is not always possible. Credit Cards are not accepted. **Hours:** 11am-9pm, Mon-Sat, 11am-6pm, Sun. **Price Range:** $, **Bus Lines:** 103, 104, 207, 402.

Harbor Palace Seafood Restaurant

4275 Spring Mountain Road in Chinatown Plaza (253-1688) – Are you looking for good, reasonably priced dim sum? If you are, well, have I found the place for you! For those who don't know what dim sum is, it's basically a series of Chinese appetizers served in hot tins. These tins are served on carts by elderly Chinese women who are seen running amongst the tables like entrants in a rickshaw race. Hyper-attentive doesn't even begin to describe their service. If you so much as make eye contact with them they will be all over you throwing the tins of dim-sum on your table. The best way to solve this dilemma is to place your hand over the bill that they stamp for the dim sum – they'll get the message. This symbolic gesture is really the only solution since these ladies don't understand English. For the record, dim sum might be considered appetizers, but after a few tins you'll be stuffed. The cheapest dim-sum includes the Beef Ball, Sweet & Sour Won Ton and Steamed BBQ Pork Bun (four in each tin). Spend a little more and you can have the Eggplant with Shrimp or Vegetarian Dumplings, the Sesame Shrimp Roll, Sugar Cane Shrimp or the terrific Pan Fried Shrimp in Rice Noodle Roll. They're served piping hot, so the minute they're put on the table, dig in! **Hours:** 10am-5am, daily. **Price Range:** $-$$, **Bus Lines:** 104, 203.

Togoshi Ramen

855 E. Twain Avenue at Swenson Avenue (737-7003) – Sadly, when people think of ramen, it's often in the form of the pre-packaged kind that is loaded with MSG and other unhealthy additives. If that's your frame of reference for ramen, than this place will be a fine surprise. Togoshi Ramen has long been a favorite of those in the know. The Ramen is terrific — my friends cannot tell me enough about the Miso Corn Tobata Ramen — pork, egg, beef, and corn thrown into a big bowl of sinuous, chewy noodles ($8). When I finally tried it, I asked for a second order to go. The dinner specials are the real deal. You can get a bowl of Saimin with a rice plate and miso soup, and of course, green tea, for only $6.50. Appetizers like cold tofu or Japanese pickles are under $4. This place has really found its groove in the last year or so, and if it's convention time it might get packed pretty quickly, but make the effort to eat here. Credit Cards are not accepted. **Hours:** 11am–10pm, daily. **Price Range:** $$, **Bus Line:** 108, 203, 213.

Prommares

6362 W. Sahara Avenue at Torrey Pines Road (221-9644) – This unique Thai restaurant has the distinction of the owner organically growing some of her ingredients (basil, lemon grass) in the backyard of her house. Your best bets are the lunch specials. Have your choice of any Chicken, Pork or Beef dish because they're all the same price ($6). Mint Leaves with Chili, Spicy Garlic, and the Pan Woon Sen (pan-fried glass noodle with eggs and onions) are your best bets for dinner. All lunch specials are served with egg rolls and rice. Credit Cards are not accepted. **Hours:** 11am–9:30pm, daily. **Price Range:** $$, **Bus Line:** 204.

Sky Dragon

4110 S. Maryland Parkway, #32 at Flamingo Road (699-9579) – This restaurant is one of the best deals in town for good, cheap Chinese food. It's a little disarming at first; their decor is no frills all the way. There are the obligatory pictures of characters representing Chinese Astrology, a few paintings of Chinese art scattered around the room, and lunch specials advertised on big, neon colored paper taped to the window. If these reasons prevent you from going in, then you have my deepest sympathies. For under $4, you can get lunch specials complete with big portions of Mongolian beef, or Chicken Lo Mein with veggies, rice, and green tea. The dinner entrees are just as reasonable: there's beef or chicken fried rice, spicy eggplant or choy sum over crab meat, and the delicious Beef with Chinese mushrooms or black bean sauce (all under $10). Afterwards, you can wash it down with a tall, refreshing glass of Thai Iced Coffee. **Hours**: 11am-9pm, daily. **Price Range**: $$, **Bus Lines:** 109*, 202*.

Pho So 1

4745 W. Spring Mountain Road at Decatur Boulevard (252-3934) – Pho is Vietnamese for a big bowl with noodles, beef, and veggies — all in a tangy broth — and it's incredibly filling for the price. You can get a variety of Pho ranging from beef ball to their combo that has everything from steak, brisket, tendon and tripe, and it's a meal unto itself. Also available is the Chao (Porridge) and the Bun-Bun (Vermicilli), which is served with beef or pork. For dessert there's a charming quirk left over from that country's colonial days —

French pastries. You can wash it all down with some rich Vietnamese coffee. It might be a little out of the way, but definitely worth the trek if you're a Pho lover (if not, you soon will be). **Hours:** 9am-10pm, daily. **Price Range:** $-$$, **Bus Line:** 203.

Pho Chien Restaurant

3839 W. Sahara Avenue, # 1 at Valley View Boulevard (873-8749) – Many of my Vietnamese friends swear this is the best eatery in town that represents their homeland's cuisine. Having been here a few times myself, I'm ready to believe them. Chein's Pho has a saltier broth than the others', but still hits the spot after a long day out on the town. The biggie is the "Pho Dac Biet", or the soup with everything – slices of steak, well-done brisket, flank and tendons, as well as veggies ($5.95) and it's quite satisfying. It's also the most expensive of the soups, so if this sounds too much for you then try the smaller entrees. Rice dishes are cheap and hearty, ranging from the relatively simple "Com Bi Cha" (shredded pork and egg loaf with steamed rice), to my favorite, "Com Tay Cam", a rich bowl of fried rice with chicken and mushrooms served in a huge clay pot ($6.95). Other dinners include Catfish, Sauteed Shrimp, Squid (yes, steamed rice and green tea are included), but none of these entrees are over $10. Quiet and homey, the décor and trimmings elevates this Vietnamese restaurant above the others, but given its' popularity, it can get a little crowded during the lunchtime as business patrons in the area rush in, but you can usually find a seat. **Hours:** 9:30am-9pm, daily. **Price Range:** $-$$, **Bus Lines:** 104, 204.

Sam Woo BBQ Restaurant

4215 Spring Mountain Road, Unit B-101 in Chinatown Plaza (368-7628) – Hong Kong-styled BBQ right here in Las Vegas. You can order at the front of the restaurant, where you can see everything being prepared right in front of your eyes. In fact, the pork hangs off the meat hooks and is carved right in front of you! Those who've been to Hong Kong or San Francisco's Chinatown know that this is *the* tradition. If you're hungry, you can try a tremendous combo plate of pork, chicken and roast duck for just $18. If you're not in the mood for all that, you can stick with a small plate of any choice of one meat mentioned above for just $5.50. Traditional Chinese food is also served here, and it's adequate, if not exactly their specialty. Lo Mein, Beef with Black Bean or Oyster Sauce, Pork, Shrimp, or Vegetable Fried Rice and other familiar staples are under $10. Credit Cards are not accepted. **Hours:** Dining - 10am-5am, daily, Take Out - 10am-10pm. **Price Range**: $$-$$$, **Bus Line:** 203.

Thai Original BBQ Restaurant

1424 S. 3rd Street at Utah Avenue (383-1128, 384-8264), 4180 S. Jones Boulevard at Flamingo Road (222-0375) – A hole-in-the wall to be sure, and one that could use a fresh coat of paint, but filled with enough good food at reasonable prices that such lack of décor can be ignored. As with most restaurants I've mentioned in this book, they have excellent lunch specials. Between 10am-3pm, you can have anything from Thai BBQ Spare Ribs, the Pepper Steak and the apparent favorite of most people I know, the very spicy Chili Chicken, for under $5. For dinner, you should look into their house specials. The best of them include Rama Shrimp

(Shrimp cooked in cream sauce and served with broccoli,) Honey Duck, and my favorite, the Dearest Crab (crab meat, shrimp, chicken and pork, and clear noodle, deep fried in a tender batter). All these dishes are served with their excellent shrimp fried rice. For rounders, order the Thai Iced Tea or Thai Iced Coffee ($1.50). **Hours:** Both Restaurants - 10am-9:30pm, daily. **Price Range:** $-$$, **Bus Lines:** 3rd - 301*, 302* (just walk a block and a half west), Jones – 102, 202*.

Middle-Eastern & Persian

Dosa-Den

3430 E. Tropicana Avenue, Suite 3-4 at Pecos Road (456-4920) – A must for those of you who are health conscious and prefer vegetarian dishes, because that's what Dosa-Den serves — pure veggie dishes — and good ones too. The Dosai (Rice Crepes) come with anything from potatoes and onion ($4.50), to vegetable mix and hot chutney ($5.50). Traditionalists will probably enjoy the curries. I especially enjoy the Vegetable Korma and Palek Paneer. Uthappam, an Indian style pancake, made from ground rice and lentils, is one of their best-known dishes. Your choice of Onion and Hot Chili, Vegetable, Coconut (my favorite) or Chick Peas, are tasty, healthy foods and are served with coconut chutney and Sambar (a spicy lentil vegetable soup with a touch of sour Tamarind). Rice Dishes, Naan and Paratha Breads, and other side dishes are also available. Beverages include Masala Iced Tea and Falooda, a delicious concoction of Rose Ice Cream, milk and rice noodles. The only drawback is the service. It's a little more leisurely paced than I'd like. Try not to be too impatient when you call their attention more than once for a refill of water or iced tea. Credit Cards are accepted for purchases of a $10 minimum. **Hours:** 11am-10pm, daily. **Price Range: $$, Bus Lines:** 111, 201*.

Ghandi's India Cuisine

4080 Paradise Road at Flamingo Road (734-0094) – For just $7.45, ($8.95 on weekends) you can stuff yourself to lengths your stomach didn't know it could go! Among the items you can choose from: Basmah Rice with veggies, Spinach Lamb, Chicken Curry, Tandoori Chicken, Vegetables Pakora, salads, soups and much more. The lunch buffet runs from 11pm–2:30pm. Don't worry about reserving a table, this restaurant has a 200 plus seating capacity even when it's busy (generally between Noon-1pm, when all the employees from near-by businesses rush in for lunch) you should still be lucky enough to get a seat. **Hours**: Lunch — 11am-2:30pm, Dinner – 5pm-10:30pm, daily. **Price Range**: $$-$$$, **Bus Lines:** 108, 202*.

House of Kabob

4110 S. Maryland Parkway, Suite #21-23 at Flamingo Road (732-2285) – A nice, collegiate, roomy place to eat for some dependable Middle Eastern food. They have the traditional options: Falafels, Greek Salads, Gyros, dips like Hummus, Babagahoush, Spinach Pie, etc., all of which cost under $5. They have a good variety for dinners. Their Mousakka, a layered eggplant dish with ground beef and potatoes covered with kefaletiri cheese, gets good reviews according to word of mouth. The all-you-can-eat soup (it's more often lentil than not), and salad isn't a bad deal. For something more traditional, have a generous helping of the

Greek Gyro Plate, Rotating Beef, or Lamb Combination, with your choice of rice or fries. The service is quick, and the seating capacity is comfortable, so if you're near the University, you might want to try this place. **Hours:** 11am-10pm, Mon-Sat., Noon-8 pm, Sun. **Price Range:** $$, **Bus Lines:** 109*, 202*, 213.

Shalimar's

3900 Paradise Road at Flamingo Road (796-0302) – Like Ghandi's, the main reason to come here is for the lunch buffet, Mon.-Fri., 11:30am-2:00pm. It's a little cheaper – $8, and the variety of food is similar to Ghandi's buffet (salads, Naan bread, Vegetable Pakoras, Tandoori Chicken, Lamb Samosa), but it's a smaller place. You gain a little in intimacy, but the tables also fill up quicker. That said, most Indians I know like the food here because "it doesn't make too many concessions to non-Indians." The décor is very attractive and they have among the most attentive waiters I've ever seen – your cup of coffee, glass of iced tea or water rarely goes unfilled. **Hours:** 11:30-2:30pm, & 5:30-10:30pm, Mon-Sat. **Price Range:** $$-$$$, **Bus Lines:** Paradise – 108, 203, 213.

India Palace

505 E. Twain Avenue at Swenson Avenue (796-4177) – Generally considered one of the better Indian lunch buffets in town. It's $7.50 on the weekdays, $8.50 on the weekends. They have a wide selection of foods, like chicken, goat, lamb, and various vegetarian dishes – with fresh Naan bread delivered to your table free of charge upon request. However, the dinners are the real show. Start with some of the excellent appetizers: the Kashmiri Nan (baked leavened bread with cashews, cherries, pistachios and raisins), or the Chicken Pakora (chicken slices dipped in garbonzo bean batter and deep fried). Then move on to the Fish Tikki Masala (Tandoori fish cubes simmer in tomato sauce), or Karahi Chicken (tender chicken stir-fried with bell-pepper, onion, tomatoes and spices). Are you in the mood for Vegetarian? No problem! All veggie dinners clock under $10. The word is that the Aloo Baingan (potatoes and eggplant in a spicy gravy), or the Navratan Korma (mixed vegetables with homemade cheese in a mild cream sauce with cashews, almonds and raisins) are first-rate. The atmosphere is a bit stiff, but the food is so good that this can be ignored. **Hours**: Lunch – 11am–2:30pm, Dinner - 5pm–10pm, daily. **Price Range**: $$-$$$, **Bus Lines**: 108, 203.

American Food

Chicago Hot Dogs

1078 N. Rancho Drive at Washington Avenue (647-3647) – I don't know what it is about this place. It could hardly look more prosaic, with the usual greasy spoon décor of redundant sports memorabilia (you guessed it, lots of posters on the Chicago Cubs, Bears and Bulls). Fortunately, the hot dogs, burgers and sandwiches are all first-rate. I recommend the Jordan Dog, a very HOT dog. Better yet, try the Italian Beef Sandwich, which has a ¼ pound of roast beef, with sweet peppers on hot Gonnella bread. This place is popular for good reason. It's very close to the Nevada State Museum and Lorenzi Public Park making lunch here a useful idea if you've been visiting either of those places. Credit Cards are not accepted. **Hours:** 11am–8pm, daily. **Price Range:** $, **Bus Lines:** 106, 208.

The Golden Eagle Restaurant

2202 Paradise Road at Sahara Avenue (737-3888) – If you're looking for a first-rate breakfast near the strip, I suggest the Golden Eagle. Try their omelet specials that are served with fresh home fries, toast and a glass of juice (your choice of orange, grapefruit or tomato — and that's a regular size, not a shot glass!), or how about their ham steak with three eggs and home fries? If you feel like a glutton, try the "Joe's Special Omelet", complete with fresh spinach, ground chunks of beef, and onions. I should also add that the lilting décor, from the old San Francisco styled ceiling lamps, and its burgundy shrouded design (tablecloth, curtains, carpeting, napkins, upholstery of the booths etc.), to the adjustable wooden shutters, made this one of the more attractive greasy spoons I've come across in the city. **Hours:** 7am-10pm, daily. **Price Range:** $$, **Bus Lines:** 108, 204.

Mr. Grill

3300 S. Decatur Boulevard, #1 at Desert Inn Road (368-4999) – One of the *best* greasy spoons in town. The interior is just what you'd expect: small seating capacity (about 16 people and that's pushing it), that classic red & white checkerboard tile, stacks of bread, tins of flour, containers of condiments near the back of eatery, and space so cramped you can hear every line of conversation in the kitchen. Haven't these always been the charms of a good greasy spoon? If you don't mind these distractions, then you're in for a treat. Mr. Grill offers very affordable "finger foods" that are generous in portion and cheap. It might be heavy on the high-fat content, but if that's not your concern then by all means dip into the menu. Among the raves: a huge portion of Chili Fries topped with dripping melted cheddar cheese, or a plate of spicy garlic fries. If you're in the mood for something more, the hot subs like Meatball Parmesan with Provolone, Corned Beef or Pastrami Rueben on Rye (with Swiss Cheese, 1000 Island & Kraut), or their delicious Crab Melt on Rye, will definitely hit the spot. They have daily lunch specials that include some of these sandwiches, appetizers and a cup of soda. Daily soups, burgers and pizza, etc. are also served. From here I'll stop and leave it up to your judgement. It would simply take too long to list everything they serve that I like. Credit Cards are not accepted. **Hours:** 6:30am-10pm, Mon-Thurs & Sat, 6:30am-11pm, Sat, Closed Sun. **Price Range:** $, **Bus Stop:** 103.

Liberty Café

2797 S. Maryland Parkway at Karen Avenue (892-9222) — There was a panic among the locals recently when we heard that the Liberty Café was moving from it's downtown home to something slightly more upscale and larger. Would the food portions be smaller, and the prices higher? Not to worry, Liberty's fine reputation for the past four decades as having cheap, first-rate breakfasts continue untarnished. Homemade country biscuits with red-eye gravy, *real* corned beef hash and two eggs with a *huge* slab of home fries (not the shoestring patty kind!) and toast, or their Trout and two eggs — are all satisfying. Lunch is decent too, try the godzillasize ½ pound Texas Burger. It's a barbecued patty topped with bacon & cheese served with your choice of baked potato or fries (a generous portion, trust me). **Hours:** 24 hrs a day, daily, 365 days a year! **Price Range:** $-$$, **Bus Line:** 109.

The Skillet Café

3999 W. Charleston Boulevard at Valley View Boulevard (877-9083) – Another entry in the rich and heavy sweepstakes. Skillet Café looks as their name suggests: counter seating, booths with shopworn vinyl padding, the usual pictures of 1950s pop icons on the wall (Marilyn, Elvis, James Dean, etc.), but their breakfasts get the biggest endorsements from locals – especially the omelets. The green chili 'n cheese and the Swiss cheese, spinach and mushroom are my favorites. All breakfasts are served with their delicious home fries and a hot buttered biscuit. **Hours:** 7am-4pm, Mon-Fri, 7am-2pm, Sat, 8am-2pm, Sun. Credit Cards are not accepted. **Price Range:** $-$$, **Bus Lines:** 104, 206*.

New York City Pizza

4440 S. Maryland Parkway at Harmon Avenue (399-2288) – Easily the snazziest pizza joint in the city. Crammed with distinctive visuals of bygone Americana like lava lamps, non-sequitur signs (Look Out Below!), corporate products, old film fanzines used for wallpaper and the like, this place really grooves with it's multi textural designs, fun pop music (anything from the Beach Boys to Roxy Music) and delicious pizza. Fresh, hot and doughy (or crispy if you like) New York City Pizza covers all the ground in what you could want in

Pizza. You need proof? Try their famous King Kong (10 lbs., 17" x 26"!) which has all the toppings ranging from anchovies to bratwurst sausage. They also serve the usual standbys like sandwiches and chicken wings, and although they're good, it's the pizza that should be first on your list. **Hours:** 11am–11pm, Sun-Thurs, 11am–Midnight, Fri-Sat. **Price Range: $$-$$$, Bus Lines:** 109*, 213.

Brat Works

4755 S. Maryland Parkway north of Tropicana Avenue (891-0008) – One of the more unique eateries near the University. It's basically a sausage eatery, but the weenies are large (1/3 lb.) and tasty and judging by the clientele, very popular with students and faculty. You can have your choice of German Bratwurst, Cajun Sausage or the tangy Spanish Chorizo, smothered with your choice of grilled onions, sauerkraut, cheese or chili (50¢ extra). Wash it down with some beer (standard variety, Foster's, Becks, etc.) and you'll feel pretty heavy as you head back to class. **Hours:** 11am–10pm, daily. **Price Range: $, Bus Lines:** 109*, 201*.

Mugshots

3342 S. Sandhill Road at Desert Inn Road (454-6100) – If you're the kind of person that craves greasy fish'n'chips, then this is the stop for you. Every Wednesday afternoon and evening, this energetic, cozy little joint has their all-you-can-eat fish and chips special for just $6. Other great items include their clams steamed in garlic beer broth, their delicious mini-burgers, and their Sunday special — Peel & Eat Shrimp for just 35¢ a piece. The crowd favorite remains their Chicago Beef Sandwich, which has mounds of Italian Beef piled to the sky on a Gonella Roll, and served with a side of au jus or hot pepper sauce. **Hours:** 24 hours, daily. **Price Range:** $-$$, **Bus Lines:** 112.

Huntridge Drugstore Restaurant

1122 E. Charleston Boulevard at Maryland Parkway (384-3737) – Located inside the Huntridge Drugstore on eastside of town, the Huntridge Restaurant is a companion to the historic Huntridge Theater located right across the street. Established in 1948, the Huntridge Restaurant hasn't added much to their interior in the last 50 years, yet customers still come here for the good food and ultra-low prices. The owners of the restaurant (although it's really an open-air grill with counter stools – upholstered in cherry red no less) are Bill and Doris Fong, who not only serve classic American grill food like burgers and fries, but good Chinese food too. You have to try their Chinese omelet, which, incidentally, is the *most* expensive (i.e. it's still cheap) breakfast item on the menu. Especially rich in taste are the big stack pancakes or French toast, and you can hardly go wrong with their breakfast special – bacon and eggs with hash browns and toast (sounds light, eeh?). The lunch menu offers classics like chicken fried steak with brown gravy, and grilled beef liver with onions and bacon. The best of the Chinese menu is anything from a big plate of ham, pork or the shrimp fried rice and you'll get a generous helping. The best thing about this place is the service. Like the classic, vintage American diners of old – it's fast! Credit Cards are not accepted. **Hours:** 8am-6pm, Mon-Sat, 9am-2pm, Sun. **Price Range:** $, **Bus Lines:** 109*, 206*.

Peppermill Restaurant & Lounge

2985 Las Vegas Boulevard South (735-4177) – Tucked behind the Riviera hotel and lying slightly aslant off the famous strip is the Peppermill. This place has been a Vegas standard since it opened in 1972 and the stylish, vintage décor grabs your attention immediately: in the middle of the room there's a fireplace near a shallow pool with a gas pipe in the middle that causes the flames to appear as though they are dancing on the surface of the water. Low sofas line the mirrored walls that enticingly reflect the flames. You'll eat in huge, over-sized booths which are surrounded by thick stalls that reach the mirrored ceiling, and the tables are draped with funky deep mauves and blues, but it's not just the interior design that keeps the customers coming back. The food here is great and servings are generous in portion. Although they serve great basic diner fare (eggs and pancakes for breakfast, cheeseburger and fries for lunch, etc.), the desserts, namely the sundaes (enjoy mounds of whipped cream on top of large scoops of chocolate ice cream as two bananas bestride the massive creation with sticky fudge dripping down its' sides), and fruit plates (which come with an entire pineapple, two bananas and a whole, sliced orange among other tropical treats, resembling a hat prop for an old Carmen Miranda musical) are my favorites. As for the drinks, the "Scorpion" – six shots of various liquors served in a 64-ounce oversized brandy – is a must. Regulars have been frequenting this place for nearly 30 years, so it's a fair guess that the Peppermill must be doing something right. **Hours**: It's on the strip – so like everything else on the road - 24 hours a day and seven days a week. **Price Range**: $$, **Bus Line**: 301*, 302*.

Italian

Ferraro's

5900 W. Flamingo Road west of Decatur Boulevard (364-5300) – Many of my Italian-American friends rave about this place to no end. It's generally regarded as one of the best Italian restaurants in the city, and it wouldn't be in this book if weren't affordable — in fact it's one of the most reasonably priced "four-star" restaurants in the city. Jump right in with the appetizers: mozzarella caprese, fried calamari, traditional antipasto, soup du jour and any of the salads — house, caesar, spinach or tomato with onion. There are 8-inch personal pizzas, spagetti marinara with meatballs, lasagna, ravioli, manicotti, eggplant parmigiana and pastas with your choice of marinara, bolognese and Alfredo sauces (all under $8). Also, appetizers like potato croquettes with roasted peppers are a must. The restaurant is quiet and nicely atmospheric, with accompanying music to go with the food. On Thursday nights they have guest singers doing their best Frank Sinatra and Dean Martin imitations – they say it's the sincerest form of flattery. This is a popular place so you might want to call ahead for reservations just to be on the safe side. **Hours:** Flamingo – 5:30pm-10:30 pm, Sun-Thurs, 5:30pm-11pm, Fri-Sat. **Price Range:** $$-$$$, **Bus Lines:** 102, 202*.

Capozzoli's

3333 S. Maryland Parkway at Desert Inn Road (731-5311) – A suprisingly suave, hip ristorante that's affordable. It has a mirror-paneled dining room with plants and statuettes serving as dividers for the 180-seat capacity, and you'll get a kick out of the photos of celebrities lining the walls.

The lunch specials (11-3 pm) are a bargain. Tasty Romaine Salad with Italian vinaigrette, or Chicken Pastina Soup served with their crusty, freshly baked Italian bread are under $4. They have huge sandwiches like meatball, sausage, or steak with pepper, which are served with fries. If you're in the mood for some classic entrees, try the cheese or meat ravioli, egg-plant, chicken, or veal parmigiana with spagetti (with red or white clam sauce), or simple classic pastas like linguine with meatballs or marinara. You can top all this off with some coffee and classic Italian desserts like spumoni or tortoni. **Hours**: 24 hours a day, daily. **Price Range: $$, Bus Lines:** 109*, 112.

Fortunato's Italian Restaurant

3430 E. Tropicana Avenue at Pecos Road (458-3333) – You can have a simple, candlelight dining experience at Fortunato's. The fresh, hot, complimentary bread kicks your meal off on a positive note. For lunch, I like to have a hot sandwich, my favorite being the Rib eye steak and mush-rooms. The Calzones are also very tempting. Their pizzaburger, cheese & meatball, or the pizzaburger, cheese & sausage are enough to last you the whole day. The dinner entrees include the full, and I mean *full*, order of pasta of your choice: linguine, mestaccioli, shells, cappalini, or rigatoni, with a full range of sauces: the butter parsley, the mushroom garlic, and their popular, heaven-sent, alla angelo, which is a heady mixture of artichoke, mushroom, black ol-ives and pimentos. All pasta dinners are served with soup or salad. Care to really dig in? The house specialties include the Gnocci – miniature dumplings made with potato and semolina wheat, rolled in marinara sauce with Romano cheese; and the Cannelloni — home made egg pasta rolled and filled with chopped veal, chicken, beef, and pork which is then blended with spinach, carrots and onions, topped with mozzarella cheese and meat sauce. Dinners come with soup or salad and a side of pasta. Finish the evening with some dessert, if you have room for it, with some rum cake or cannoli — the classic Italian dessert (you've seen it in all the mob movies) that's a pastry shell filled with sweetened ricotta cheese and chocolate chips. **Hours:** 11am-10 pm, Mon-Fri, 5pm-10pm, Sat, Closed Sun. **Price Range**: $$-$$$, **Bus Lines:** 111, 201*.

Chicago Joe's

820 S. 4th Street at Carson Street (382-5637) – A popular local eatery for nearly 25 years. Joe's is a comfortable little restaurant set in an old, brick-layered residential house in the heart of downtown. For lunch try the Submarine Sandwich. It's loaded with Genoa salami, ham, pepperoni, mozzarella, onion, lettuce, tomato and Italian dressing. The dinner choices are endless, but I've always enjoyed their Veal Picante and Cioppini. All dinners are served with bread and your choice of soup or salad. If you do choose their salad, I implore you to try the homemade Cream Garlic Dressing. **Hours**: 11am–10pm, Mon-Thurs, 11am–11pm, Fri-Sat, Closed Sun. **Price Range: $$-$$$, Bus Lines**: 206*, 207.

Roxy's Pipe Organ Pizzeria at the Fiesta Hotel & Casino

2400 N. Rancho Drive at Carey Road (631-7000) – This pizzeria features thin crusted pies, pastas, a first-rate antipasto bar and a variety of Italian gelati. It's worth coming here for the food alone, but the Roxy is especially commanding on Thursday nights when you can catch silent films played with a backdrop of an astonishingly huge pipe organ. This organ was first installed at the Roxy Theater in New York City in 1927 and has over 2,500 pipes, three consoles, and a 60-horsepower turbine engine to supply the wind. The results are a combination of sound effects that are unbounded, and at times even thrilling. Classic silent comedies starring Harold Lloyd and Buster Keaton are amusing in themselves, but especially so when the organist plays the dramatic chords that accompany a climax in an action sequence. The films are shown on the hour, and they last around 20-25 minutes. Even if you don't have the good fortune to drop in on a Thursday night, the organist will play anything from classical (Bach) to Broadway (Phantom), and even takes requests from the audience. Seating capacity in this barn-like restaurant is close to 600, so don't worry about seating. All in all, grand entertainment, good food and a rousing atmosphere will make the Roxy a destination worth seeking out. **Hours**: 4-10pm, daily **Price Range**: $-$$, **Bus Lines**: 101, 206 (but you're better off driving here because these bus lines run only once an hour.)

Metro Pizza

4001 S. Decatur Boulevard at Flamingo Road (362-7896), 2250 E. Tropicana Avenue at Eastern Avenue (736-1955), see phone book for more listings – One of the best pizza chains in town. It's run by some guys from Chicago named "John" and "Sam", and they apparently brought some of the best pizza recipes with them. A large (18") pizza will *comfortably* feed two people. Among the varieties: The Honolulu (Canadian bacon, pineapple, onions, green peppers, bacon bits) or the Casa Verde (A veggie pizza with mushrooms, green peppers, black olives, broccoli and tomatoes). For the more adventuresome pizza eater, the "specialty" pizzas will be your choice. A large (18") will *easily* feed two people. The ones to try: The Memphis (BBQ-Chicken pizza toped with red onions) the Boston (Clams, garlic, bread crumbs, bacon bits and mozzarella cheese) and the El Paso (Chili, jalapenos, olives, tomatoes, onions, sour cream and mozzarella cheese). Do you want to go all out? The stuffed pizzas are another choice. The large (16") is made with two layers of cheese and dough and will easily feed *three* people. Among the standouts: The Stockyard (mounds of pepperoni, sausage and ground beef), the Chicago (sautéed spinach between layers of melted mozzarella cheese) the South Side (a rich blend of three cheeses – mozzarella, ricotta and romano). Ffinally, there's the most popular house item, the Pasta Pie (Mozzarella, ricotta cheese, ziti noodles and tomato sauce). The restaurant's interior is a bit sterile. Maybe it pushes too hard with the fifties nostalgia, but if starkness in period décor is the biggest of Metro's problem, you probably don't have much to worry about. **Hours**: All Branches – 11am-10pm, Sun-Thurs, 11am-1pm, Fri-Sat. **Price Range:** $$-$$$, **Bus Lines:** Flamingo – 111, 202*, Decatur – 103, 202*, Tropicana – 110, 201*.

Hispanic Flavors

Lindo Michoacan

2655 E. Desert Inn Road east of Eastern Avenue (735-6828) – Easily one of the most adventurous Mexican restaurants in the city. What sets Lindo apart from the competition is not just the fine quality, but the unique variety of cuisine they offer. Lengua a la Michoacan (fresh beef tongue with tomato and jalapeno), or Milanesa con Papa (fresh goat!) may sound off-putting but they're well presented and tasty. Even the more standard fare like burritos and tortas have a unique taste to them. Throw in a festive atmosphere with a live Tejano band playing in the dining room and you've got yourself a fun experience. **Hours**: 11am–10pm, Mon-Wed, 11am–11pm, Thurs-Fri, 9:30am–11pm, Sat-Sun. **Price Range**: **$$-$$$**, **Bus Lines**: 110, 112.

Florida Café at the Howard Johnson Hotel

1401 Las Vegas Boulevard South north of Charleston Boulevard (385-3013) – Now here's an unsung highlight. A small, Cuban-styled restaurant that's located inside the Howard Johnson located right on the Boulevard. The prices are moderate; the food is very good. If you enjoy authentic Cuban cuisine, try their Bolicho Mechadò (rump roast stuffed with sausage), the Costillas Empanizada (breaded ribs), Distec Criollo (Cuban country style steak, a very robust flavor, and just on the right side of tender), or the Bacalao a la Vizcaina (codfish with red sauce) . All dinners are served with white rice and black beans. A daily lunch special that highlights any of the above dishes is only $5. If you're in the mood for something lighter, try a bowl of black bean, red bean, or chicken soup, which are all under $3. They hit the spot and you get complimentary bread, too. A very attentive staff only adds to the appeal. **Hours:** 7am-10pm, daily. **Price Range: $$ Bus Line:** 301*.

Rincon Criollo

1145 Las Vegas Boulevard South at Charleston Boulevard (388-1906) – A decent stop for budget travelers when strolling on the boulevard is this Cuban restaurant. Compared to its more festive competitor just a few blocks south, this place is a bit blah in terms of décor and the tight seating capacity (about 25 customers at best) can be a drawback. If you can look beyond these shortcomings, then you're in for a good meal. Rincon does offer some quick, tasty "budget" (under $5) dishes like the Avocado Salad, The Vegetable Sandwich, or a simple bowl of hot, tasty Black Bean Soup. If you're a little more ambitious, try the Cuban Styled Country Steak, or Ground Beef with Olives. The meals are served with a generous portion of white rice and black beans. The Cuban desserts are the real treats. You can have your choice of Guava Shells, Papaya Chunks, or Shredded Coconut served with a very rich portion of cream cheese. **Hours:** 11am-10pm, daily. **Price Range:** $-$$, **Bus Lines:** 206*, 301.

Casa Don Juan

1202 S. Main Street south of Charleston Boulevard (384-8070) – This lively little restaurant is a little out of the way, but it's certainly worth seeking out. Casa offers some very good lunch specials for just $5: Red Chili Verde (just the right touch of chili powder kick), Beef or Chicken Fajitas, and Pork Carnitas. They're all served with the soup of the day, rice, beans, tortillas, and a nice variety of salsa. The combo dinners are a fine choice. Anything from Red Chili Beef, Chicken Steak, Steak Ranchero and the ever popular tongue in green sauce. It's all served with rice and beans. One more thing, I dare you to resist their thick Mexican milk shakes! It's a tall glass of any of the following flavors: strawberry, papaya, mango, banana, melon, mamey and guanavana – and they are made with real fruit chunks. A spunky atmosphere is well produced with engaging props (piñatas, sombrero, panchos), plants freshening up the room and some fun mariachi music playing through the speakers. The waitresses are not exactly fluent in English, so please be patient when you give your order. **Hours**: 8am-10pm, daily. **Price Range**: $$, **Bus Lines**: 105, 206.

La Mexicana Deli

3675 S. Decatur Boulevard, #1 at Twain Avenue (252-7857) – A terrific Mexican eatery that serves hot, rich foods cheap. You can have tacos, a *huge* bowl of Menudo or a variety of burritos (I recommend the chili verde). Their specialty is their burrito supreme and it's a meal onto itself as it's loaded with chicken, beef, onions, tomatoes, beans, rice, sour cream and guacamole all wrapped up in two flour tortillas. For the same price, you can dig into the combo plate. You'll get chili, a taco, tamale, a chili releno and an enchilada. Finally, if you're a fajita fan, they're hot and delicious here, with your choice of chicken or beef, served with onions and green peppers. Believe me, food this good and this cheap is to be treasured. No Credit Cards are accepted.

Hours: 9am-10pm, Mon-Sat, Closed Sun. **Price Range:** $, **Bus Line:** 103.

The El Steak Burrito

4590 Spring Mountain Road east of Decatur Boulevard (871-9082) – This little hole-in-the-wall has been a favorite for many people who live on the westside of town. Like many small eateries, the décor is minimal (although there are piñatas and sombreros pinned to the wall for "ambience"), the seating capacity is small (15 people tops) and the menu isn't too varied. But as their name implies, they serve steak burritos – and boy are they delicious – loaded with mounds of ground beef, onions, tomatoes, cheese and lettuce and wrapped in two layers of tortillas. Their breakfast specials are pretty good too, most notably the Chorizo and Sausage burrito. Even the side dishes are generous with a big portion of Spanish rice and a plate of Refried Beans for just 85¢. Incidentally, nothing on the menu is over $4. The owner, a lovely Mexican woman named Maria, is extremely friendly, just be careful if she's watching her soap operas on Univision near the front counter – you might have to ring the service bell a few times to get her attention! Credit Cards are not accepted. **Hours:** 7am-3 pm, Mon-Sat, Closed Sun. **Price Range:** $, **Bus Line:** 203.

Paco's Hideaway at the Sahara Hotel

2535 Las Vegas Boulevard South at Sahara Avenue (737-2111) – One of the more moderately priced restaurants on the strip. The menu isn't the most adventurous, but entrees like a Burrito Platter, Chimichanga, and the Taco Salad are good. They also serve margaritas for just 99¢. They have a spacious dining area that's fairly intimate, especially for a casino hotel. It tends to be empty, and that's a shame, because the food and service here are really worthwhile. **Hours:** 5pm-10pm, daily. **Price Range:** $$, **Bus Lines:** 108, 204, 301*, 302*.

Other Ethnic Flavors

Horn Of Africa

1510 S. Las Vegas Boulevard at Wyoming Road (383-6741) – If you ever wanted to try Ethiopian food, then the Horn of Africa is a good place to start. It's another entry in the no frills décor department, but they offer ultra friendly service (I still can't get over that they bow to me), and certain dishes are pretty affordable. I absolutely endorse their vegetarian dishes. Yesmir Wit (pureed red lentil with spice, Yekik Alicha (yellow split peas cooked with mild curry) and Ye Atakilt Alicha (mixed vegetables with spice and curry) are very satisfying (all under $5) and include a side salad. The vegetables are presented in a big bowl and served with a delicious thin, crepe-like bread called Injera in which you roll the vegetables and eat like a sandwich. They serve some meat entrees, ranging from filet of beef to tender lamb, but the portions of meat are meager and they cost up to $5 more than the veggie dishes. Apart from the food, there's interesting (if minimal) décor with some unique travel posters featuring remarkably robust Ethiopian women, and native artifacts like pots and hats hanging on the wall. Most interesting of all is the live entertainment on Wednesday night which will be your only chance to hear traditional "somet" music in town. The excellent location, right on Las Vegas Boulevard, makes this a most convenient stop. **Hours:** Noon-3am, daily. **Price Range**: $-$$ **Bus Line:** 301*.

Café Heidelberg

610 E. Sahara Avenue at 6th Street (731-5310) – The menu includes sausage platters, schnitzels and dinner entrees which are moderately priced ($8-$15), plus a fine selection of German beer. There's also a deli and some great imported German chocolates. This is one of the oldest restaurants in the city, and despite the dated look, it's a cozy joint with friendly service –and don't forget, on Friday and Saturday nights they have live accordion music! Always check the Friday issue of the Las Vegas Review-Journals' supplement, "Neon". The Heidelberg offers some discount coupons for dinner specials in the restaurant section. **Hours**: 10am-9pm, Mon-Sat, Closed Sun. **Price Range**: $$-$$$, **Bus Line**: 204.

Casino Gluttony: Buffets, Graveyard Specials & All-You-Can Eats

It might seem unnecessary to write a section on buffets and graveyard specials. Almost every major hotel on the strip and downtown has advertisements plastered all over the city declaring that their buffets and food specials are the best. My goal is to provide you with a handy reference as to which buffets are good, because some deals are not what they seem. Some buffets in town advertise cheap prices, but are *notoriously* bad. I've seen stale rolls, eggs so runny they drip through the slotted serving spoon, and spilled food on the floor that went unnoticed for nearly an hour until I told the manager. Believe me, anything in this section is way above this standard and is a good value for your money. As for the midnight specials, I've always felt that this was one of the inherent charms of Las Vegas. Where else can you get a triple egg Denver Omelet for only 99¢ at 3am in the morning? Hey, these casinos will do anything to keep you there all night, so take advantage of it.

Sourdough Café at Arizona Charlie's

740 S. Decatur Boulevard north of Charleston Boulevard (258-5200), www.azcharlies.com – There are many specials to be had at this neighborhood casino. The highlights are the interchangeable specials. First is the all-you-can-eat Spaghetti & Meat Sauce, which includes a tossed salad and garlic bread. If that's not available, than the all-you-can-eat Fish-n-Chips will be offered, although some people feel they're a little more generous with the batter than the fish (both $3.99), from 11am-10pm daily. Sourdough Café also has a terrific Steak and Eggs special. You get a five-ounce sirloin cooked to order, two eggs, potatoes and toast ($2.49). And what casino could have any respectability if they didn't offer graveyard specials? In Charlie's case, it's the Gambler's Breakfast, and for a mere 77¢, you can choose among the following breakfasts: Ham & Eggs with hashbrowns and toast, Pancakes with bacon or sausage, toast and juice, biscuits and gravy and much more. **Hours:** Spaghetti & Fish - 11am-10pm, daily, Steak – 24 hours, daily, Graveyard – Midnight-7am, Mon-Fri. **Bus Lines:** 103. 206*.

Marco Polo at Lady Luck Casino

3rd Street and Ogden Avenue (477-3000), www.ladylucklv.com – Their "bottomless bowl of Spaghetti and Meatballs" is a great deal. It includes a house salad and bread (just what you need – more starch) for only $7.95. If you haven't guessed, bottomless refers to "all-you-can-eat". **Hours**: 5pm-11pm, Tue-Sat. **Bus Lines:** 207, 301*.

Ristorante dei Fiori at Hotel San Remo

115 E. Tropicana Avenue at Koval Lane (739-9000), www.sanremolasvegas.com – Located just two blocks east of the strip, almost directly across from the MGM, the San Remo offers a delicious Prime Rib dinner for just $5.95. This beauty is served with a salad, baked potato, vegetables, and a roll, and is available 24 hours. On the weekends they offer one of the city's better champagne brunch buffets for just $7.95. **Hours:** Rib – 24 hours, daily, Buffet – 6am-Noon, Sat-Sun. **Bus Lines:** 201*, 301*, 302*.

Fresh Market Square Buffet at Harrahs Hotel and Casino

3475 Las Vegas Boulevard South (369-5000) – A unique buffet experience for the strip. The style has a fresh, outdoor market look — the columns inside the buffet are designed like giant fruits and vegetables! Harrah's offers one of the best moderately priced buffets on the strip. There are many interactive cooking stations that can prepare anything you want (I just love a fresh burger grilled to my neurotic perfection), and much more. The dinner buffet offers prime selections like fish, poultry, pasta, a fine salad bar, and the list goes on and on. The dessert cart alone will kill you with its awesome selection! **Hours & Price:** Breakfast - $8.99, 7am-11am, Lunch - $9.99, 11:30am-3:30pm, Dinner – $14.99, 4pm-10pm. **Bus Line:** 301*, 302*.

Bacon and Eggs Special at the El Cortez Hotel

600 Fremont Street at 6th Street (385-5200), www.elcortez.com — Not too long ago, the publisher for the *Las Vegas Advisor* came to me and asked if I could recommend a cheap breakfast. He was going to spend a day with a reporter from the "USA Today". She was in town writing an article titled "Las Vegas on Zero Dollars a Day". I recommended the 99¢ breakfast special at the El Cortez. It consists of two eggs, two slices of bacon, hashbrowns and toast. He liked it. He said the reporter liked it. She took a picture of it for the article. My editor thanked me the next day – enough said. **Hours**: 24 hours, daily. **Bus Lines**: 207, 301*, 302*.

Hound Doggie's Snack Bar at the Riviera Hotel & Casino

2901 Las Vegas Boulevard South (734-5110), www.theriveria.com – 25¢, 50¢ drafts, $1.35 ¼ dogs and a huge steak sandwich for only $3.50, this is a great place to stop on the strip if you want a good, quick snack. Only drawback: adults only. **Hours**: 24 hours, daily. **Bus Lines**: 301*, 302*.

Shrimp Cocktails at Golden Gate Hotel

1 Fremont Street at Main Street (385-1906), www.goldengatecasino.com – The Golden Gate is the home of the original 99¢ shrimp cocktail. Numerous other hotels have followed suit since (Riviera, Arizona Charlie's, Gold Spike) and they offer bigger portions, but Golden Gate stills gets my nod as top of the class for one reason – the shrimp. Gate takes pride in using cold-water shrimp, as opposed to the other hotels that use warm-water shrimp. What's the difference, you ask? Cold-water shrimp is caught off the coast of Oregon, Alaska, and Iceland. These shrimps are naturally meatier, whiter, and better. The warm-water shrimp is caught off the Indian Ocean and is naturally translucent (they're treated with paprika for pink coloration), but they also tend to be saltier than their northern counterparts. Cold-water shrimp is more expensive than the warm-water kind, so all told, The Golden Gate is giving you a pretty good deal. Maybe I am being a bit persnickety, but you can't say I don't know my 99¢ shrimp cocktails! **Hours:** 24 hours, daily. **Bus Line:** 205.

Shrimp Cocktail at the Gold Spike Hotel & Casino

400 Ogden Avenue at Las Vegas Boulevard South (384-8444) – The biggest 99¢ shrimp cocktail in the city for downtown, it isn't as tasty as Golden Gate's, but its still good. The Golden Gate might serve their's in a tall tulip glass, but Gold Spike will offer you a cereal bowl! **Hours:** 24 hours, daily. **Bus Lines:** 207, 301*, 302*.

Carnival World Buffet at Rio Suites Hotel & Casino

3700 W. Flamingo Road at Valley View Boulevard (252-7757), www.playrio.com – One of the best in the city. The delicious food hails from a variety of countries (hence the name Carnival World) and they spare no expense with the keen décor. Cuisine from Brazil, Mexico, America, Italy and Asia are prepared in separate kitchens. An absolutely bright presentation only makes it more rewarding. It's just a little costlier than the other buffets in town, but man, it's worth it. **Hours & Price:** Breakfast – $8, 8:30am-10:30am, Lunch - $11, 11am-3:30pm, Dinner - $14, 3:30pm-10pm. **Bus Line:** 202*.

Paradise Buffet at Fremont Hotel & Casino

200 Fremont Street inside the Fremont Street Experience (385-3232), www.fremontcasino.com – Terrific variety, great service, and a high-end presentation makes this buffet a standout bargain for those of you staying in budget-conscious downtown. The Seafood buffet, which is offered three days a week, is a little pricey, but it's hard to resist: Swordfish, Orange Roughy, and Stuffed Shrimp are just some of the delicacies served. **Hours & Price:** Breakfast - $4.95, 7am-10:30am, Mon-Sat, Lunch - $5.95, 11am-3pm, Mon-Sat, Dinner - $9.95, 4pm-10pm, Mon, Wed & Thurs, 4pm-11pm, Fri-Sat, Seafood Buffet - $12.95, 4pm-10pm, Tue, Fri & Sun. **Bus Line:** 108, 205, 301*, 302*. (The Fremont Street Experience is all within walking distance of these bus lines.)

The Buffets at Bellagio

3600 Las Vegas Boulevard South (693-7111), www.bellagiolasvegas.com – Bellagio has a reputation for being a cut above everything else on the strip, and does it with a self-conscious air of regality. Whether you find this to your liking or not, you can't deny that this is one of the snazzier places in town where you can feast yourself toward dizzying heights. Whether it's a three-egg omelet made to order for breakfast, or international flavors (Chinese, Italian, French, and Thai) for lunch, the Bellagio has something to offer everyone. For those in the mood, the dinner buffet is even more extravagant (and expensive) at $22.95, but worth it if you've discovered on your final day that you've saved so much money (courtesy of my advice) and you want to end your trip with a grand gesture of indulgence. **Hours & Price:** Breakfast - $9.95, 7am-10:30am, Lunch - $12.95, 11am-3:30pm. **Bus Line:** 201, 301*, 302*.

Deliís and Markets

The variety of ethnic and alternative food markets has blossomed considerably in the last five years, which is not surprising when you consider the population boom and the diversity of the ethnic groups that have followed. Naturally, food markets to reflect this diversity have followed suit: New York Italian, Asian, Middle Eastern, Latin American, etc. There are numerous little markets around the valley, but I've concentrated on the biggest and best to make your legwork a little easier. The "alternative" food markets referred to here are nothing too radical (in fact, they're small chains that you might be familiar with in your hometown). They're basically health food stores and discount bakeries, but well worth the mention because of their quality and low prices.

Siena Deli

2250 E. Tropicana Avenue at Eastern Avenue (736-8424) — This deli has been a favorite of East Coast transplants for over 10 years. Imported cheese wheels and meats dangle from the ceiling with an aroma that tempts you as soon as you walk through the door. They serve almost anything you'd expect from an Italian deli: Pizza, Calzone, Pepper and Eggs, Prosciutto and other sandwiches. More than just fine Italian food, Siena has a fairly impressive array of imports from Italy and Sicily. Pastas, breads, candy, olive oil, cheeses, and spices — you name it — they have it. In the summer, nothing hits the spot like Gelato and Italian ices. The atmosphere is particularly fun. An old, native Italian who is the patriarch of the family business, has a VCR that plays old soccer matches featuring Italian teams. He watches these matches with amazing enthusiasm, screaming a string of expletives in broken English and Italian when his team isn't winning (even though these are old matches and he *knows* the outcome!). Elsewhere, tough-talking New Yorkers are forever shouting over each other – giving their orders to the servers behind the counter. Arguably the best store in town to buy imported Italian goods. **Hours:** 8:30am-6pm, Mon-Sat, 10am-4pm. **Bus Lines:** 110, 201*.

Coach's Deli

3544 Wynn Road at Spring Mountain Road (251-7872) – An excellent deli that offers some terrific daily specials. Anything from a 12" hot Meatball Sub with cheese to the 12" grilled N.Y. pastrami sub are great deals that will keep you stuffed for hours. The daily sandwich specials include a big basket of peppered fries and a drink with free refills ($6.25). You'll also love their ½ lb. patty cheeseburgers with fries and soda ($4.95). Just one squeeze and you'll watch with fascination as the mayo and French dressing drippings race with each other toward your elbow. No, it's not the healthiest item on the menu, but you already knew that! I should warn you that this place is small, it seats about 12 people at best. They make their money with deliveries, so delivery people are forever jockeying back and forth from the counter to the door. It's best to stop in and get something to go as you hit the city. **Hours:** 7am–8pm, Mon-Fri, 7am-2pm, Sat. **Bus Line:** 203.

Minuto's Italian Deli

6160 W. Tropicana Avenue at Jones Boulevard (248-0323) – A small, but pleasant stop on the westside of town. Lots of classic "New York" items like cannoli cream, Manhattan soda, meats (pepperoni, pastrami), and cheeses (ricotta, provolone) are all along the front counter. There's good dine-in food too, the best being the Mortadella & Provolone hero sandwich (under $5), and any of their pasta dinners with at least 10 different kinds of pasta (fusilli, farfalle, rigatoni, ziti, etc.) and some good sauces like clam, calamari and bolognesa, and even vodka! Served with a salad and garlic bread (under $10). **Hours:** 9am-7pm, Tue-Sat, 10am-4pm, Sun, Closed Mon. **Bus Lines:** 102, 201*.

99 Ranch Market

4155 W. Spring Mountain Road at Wynn Road (364-8899) – This is by far the biggest market of its type in Las Vegas. Anything you could want in an Asian cuisine is here. You'll get a kick out of their giant seafood section that includes fresh lobster and squid. Imported products like bento, udon, rice noodles, and a variety of candies and snacks are also sold. It's a little more expensive than many of the dozens of mom & pop Asian stores that are scattered all over the city, but the convenience of having such a large variety of products under one roof makes this place a great stop. Be sure to check out the sales shelf toward the front left when you enter the store. You can find loads of goodies like tempura batter, fishcakes, ramen, breads, etc. for 50% off. **Hours:** 9am-9pm, daily. **Bus Lines:** 203.

Relampago Cubano Market

634 N. Eastern Avenue at Bonanza Road (380-2869) – Relampago sells all sorts of spices, peppers and prepared rice dishes that are hard to find anywhere else. Remember that this is the east side of town, where the ethnic diversity is high, prices are low, and the stuff is genuine. They sell produce (malanga, boniato, and plantains), a host of Goya products (black beans and rice) and good pastries like pastelitos (a small flaky turnover filled with meat, cheese or guava, for just 70¢). Be sure to try their Jamaican soda (particularly the Ginger Beer). **Hours:** 8am-8pm, Mon-Sat, Noon-5pm, Sun. **Bus Lines:** 110, 207.

Trader Joe's

2101 S. Decatur Boulevard at O' Bannon Drive south of Oakey Boulevard (367-0227) – If you don't have one of these in your neighborhood, Joe's is a big, alternative shopping store for those of us who are a little more health-conscious and diverse in our food habits. This store is hard to beat for calorie watchers. They have a variety of low fat and low-sodium products, like rye bread, sourdough bagels, toasted cereals, cracker snacks and more. The deli is also impressive with its fat-free sausages and lean coldcuts, as well as low-fat cheeses. Trader Joe's also arguably has the best selection of healthy frozen food entrees in the city. You'll get everything from fat-free vegetable pizza (which isn't as bad as it sounds), stuffed salmon fillets, and calamari steaks. All of these products contain less than 480 MG of sodium per serving. There's an impressive selection of imported wine and beer, which is *not* for the health-conscious. Don't forget to see what's in their coffee store, there are beans culled from all over the world (Italy, France, Vietnam, etc.). Best of all, Trader Joe's has a rack near the cashiers filled with recipes (you must try their recipe for curried rice salad) and health tip information that serves your agenda for shopping in this store. **Hours:** 9am-9pm, daily. **Bus Lines:** 103, 205.

Wild Oats Community Market

3455 E. Flamingo Avenue at Eastern Avenue (434-8115), 6729 W. Sahara Avenue at Rainbow Boulevard (942-1500), www.wildoats.com – Not just content with offering some healthy alternatives for the fitness conscious (therapy bath salts, baked tofu, organic bagged veggies, vitamins, herbal chapstick, low-fat rice drinks, organic pancake and waffle mix, natural fruit sugar cookies), Oat's also has an excellent deli with a fruit salad and juice bar and a bakery with low-fat and sodium breads, rolls and pastries that taste fine. **Hours:** Both Stores – 7am-10pm, daily. **Bus Lines:** Flamingo – 110, 202*, Sahara – 101, 204.

India Sweets & Spices

5006 S. Maryland Parkway at Sahara Avenue inside Commercial Center (736-6677) – The best Indian grocery in the city. They have fresh vegetables, plus Halaal meats, a frozen food section (i.e. frozen vegetable samosa), and many Indian goods like Basmati Rice, Yellow Peas, and Coconut Milk. If you have a desire to learn more about Indian cuisine, they sell English-language cookbooks for Indian dishes. **Hours:** 11am-8pm, daily. **Bus Lines:** 109*, 201*.

Liquor

Cost Plus World Market

3840 S. Maryland Parkway at Harmon Avenue (794-2070), 2151 N. Rainbow Boulevard at Lake Mead Boulevard (638-8844), www.costplus.com – Although this well-known chain specializes in many discount products (coffee beans, jams, bread, vegetarian crackers, imported pasts) the coolest aspect of this place is the selection of imported wine, beer and ciders from all over the globe with discount deals that are much cheaper than any of the high-brow "specialty liquor" stores in town. **Hours:** Both Stores - 9am-9pm, Mon-Sat, 10am-7pm, Sun. **Bus Lines:** 109*, 213.

R.G. Liquors

4080 Paradise Road at Flamingo Road (734-2600) – A very useful place close to the strip for those of you who are looking for inexpensive beer, wine and other spirits. An added plus is a very friendly staff who know their liquor. **Hours:** 9am-9pm, Mon-Sat, 9am-5pm, Sun. **Bus Lines:** 108, 202*.

Lee's Discount Liquor

9110 Las Vegas Boulevard South at Agate Road (269-2400), 3480 E. Flamingo Road at Pecos Road (458-5700), 1780 N. Rainbow Boulevard at Oakey Boulevard (458-5700), see phone book for more listings – One of Las Vegas' oldest discount liquor chains. There's a good sale every week, with bottles being anywhere from 25%-40% cheaper than supermarket prices. Though Lee's does lack a certain variety and sophistication, major brand names like Cluny Scotch, Genny Ale Cream, Steinlager, MacNauton Canadian Whiskey, Dewars Scotch, Bailey's Irish Cream and Kahlua are available. **Hours:** 9am-11pm, Mon-Sat, 9am-9pm, Sun. **Bus Lines:** The Strip – 301*, 302*, Flamingo – 110, 202*.

Bakeries and Sweet Shops

Being that this is Las Vegas, and you've indulged in virtually all forms of gluttony, why stop at the sweet stuff? Boy, are you in for a surprise when you read what I've listed below. A smattering of good ol' fashioned bakeries, candy stores, and ice cream parlors are spread out all over the valley, so pay attention to which one might be closest to you when you're out on the town.

Great Buns Bakery

3270 E. Tropicana Avenue west of Pecos Road (898-0311) – More like a warehouse than a retail shop, but man, are their baked goods tasty! What do they have, you ask? Soft and crusty breadsticks, hot dog rolls, hamburger rolls, kaiser rolls, 7" focaccia bread, cookies, tarts, and a large variety of breads (seven-grain, rye), etc. They offer some daily specials which can be anything from a loaf of their excellent pumpernickel or cinnamon-apple bread, to baked goods like cookies or tarts up to 50% off the regular price. **Hours:** 7am–4pm, Mon-Sat, Closed Sun. **Bus Lines:** 111, 201*.

La Mexicana Bakery

3675 S. Decatur Boulevard, #1 at Twain Avenue (252-7857) – La Mexicana, as mentioned in the Restaurant chapter, is a good Mexican eatery. It's also a very good Mexican bakery. They sell a variety of baked products like cookies, hot buns, and cakes for just 40¢! **Hours:** 9am-10pm, Mon-Sat, Closed Sun. **Bus Line:** 103.

Las Vegas Jerky's, Etc., Inc.

1 South Main Street, 3rd Floor in Jackie Gaughans's Plaza Hotel & Casino (385-7991) – This small hideaway is a real treat for snack addicts, stocked with loads of goodies imported from Hawaii as well as locally produced foodstuff. You must try their delicious dried bagel chips, either the Parmesan cheese or apple cinnamon. They're packaged in 16 oz. giant tubes and for just $6 you can munch yourself silly. Other goodies include one pound bags of dried fruit like bing cherries, Turkish apricots and banana chips (all under $5). Beef jerkys are the specialty. The Islander Smoked Beef, Islander Teriyaki, and Sweet Pork jerkys are as tasty (and as sodium drenched) as jerkys go. The price is a little high (all $8.25 for a ½ pound bag) but depending on the volume packages, the more you buy the better the value. Don't forget to try their nuts and seeds. One pound bags of honey roasted almonds ($5), toffee peanuts, and pine nuts (both $3.50) are always handy snacks to have when you're hitting the slots. Four-oz. bags of Cappuccino, Cream Coffee, Yogurt Fruit, Black Coffee and Coconut candy are just $3. And people, please buy a one pound box of Karen's

Macadamian Shortbread Cookies ($6). A Higher Power created this stuff to be consumed without guilt! **Hours:** 9am – 9pm, Mon-Sat; 9am – 5pm, Sun. **Bus Lines:** 106, 205.

Freed's Bakery

4780 S. Eastern Avenue at Tropicana Avenue (456-7762) — This bakery has been voted by the Las Vegas Review-Journal's annual readers poll as the best in Vegas for nine consecutive years. Yes, it really is worth the accolades. A relatively small store, when you walk in through the entrance, you'll swear you're in the back kitchen. The last time I was there they had flour on the floor, itemized account records on the counter, and those big, pink, cake cartons stacked up along the wall. Still, on your first visit, you'll be paying too much attention to the baked goodies for this to distract you. Among the delights: Russian coffee cake, Fruit pie with Bavarian cream filled crust, and the very popular chocolate eclairs ($2.35, and so light in texture they'll float right out of your hand). An endless array of donuts, bars, and cookies ($1-$2, check out the samples in finger bowls on the top counter) that you're welcome to taste, and the variety of cheesecakes ($3 for a slice) will really sell it for you. The prices might be a little higher than other bakeries, but if you're tired of mediocre baked products that have that horrendously greasy, "crisco" aftertaste, and you'd like to indulge in something sweet, delicate and filling, then by all means treat yourself to this place, you won't be sorry. **Hours:** 7am-6pm, daily. **Bus Lines:** 110, 201*.

Luv It Frozen Custard

505 E. Oakey Boulevard east of Las Vegas Boulevard South (384-6452) – This place has been around for over 25 years. It's been around this long because it has the best frozen custard most people have ever tasted. The custard is made daily with fresh egg and cream and the prices are amazingly low for what you get. The flavors change from day to day, but vanilla, chocolate and raspberry tend to be the staples. Other flavors like butter pecan, rocky road, malt cream, Scotch crème, rum rainbow and fresh banana nut are godsends on a hot, sweltering summer day. A single scoop in a cup or cone is only $1.15, double $2.10, and the triple is only $2.70! If you're up to the challenge, the sundaes are the real treats. It's only $2.50 for a small cup, $3.40 for the large. Among my favorites: Banana Fudge Krumble (hot fudge, sliced bananas and cookie crumbs), butter crunch, hot apple walnut, and the sprinkle special (marshmallow, jimmies and chopped peanuts). The only drawback is that there is no seating area. You order through a small window, but it's hardly a hindrance, especially when most of you will be stopping in during your walk on the boulevard anyway. Just beware of the long line in the summer. The hidden treasure of downtown, for those with a sweet tooth. No Credit Cards accepted. **Hours:** 11am-10pm, Mon-Fri, Noon-11pm, Sat, 1pm-10pm, Sun. **Bus Lines:** 108, 301*, 302*.

Albina's Italian American Bakery

3035 E. Tropicana Avenue, #2 off Pecos Road (433-5400) – Recent transplants from New York swear "on their mother's grave" that this is the best Italian-American bakery in the city. Cookies like regina, biscotti sesame, pinola, and macaroon (a pound of any variety is $3.50) are begging to be bought at the front counter. Elsewhere, specialty pastries like Sicilian sponge cake with rum, canollis, and my favorite – the Fogliattelle (an unforgettable honeycomb crisp-flake pastries with cheese filling) are just $1.50-$2.25. It's a simple, no-frills décor (there is nowhere for you to sit down and munch) kind of a place. The location is a bit out of the way, but the prices are so cheap and the pastries so good, that you'll make the effort to get here. **Hours:** 8am-6pm, Mon-Sat, 8am-5pm. **Bus Lines:** 111, 201*.

Sugarless Shack

2570 E. Tropicana Avenue at Topaz Road (450-9728) – The diabetics delight for those on the eastside of town. Cookies, muffins, wafers, chocolates, syrups and my favorite – espresso fudge, plus many of the other products, use non-caloric and nutritive caloric sweeteners like Nutrasweet and Acesulfame K, Sorbitol and Fructose, and the results are baked goods that don't have any stagnant aftertaste at all. The prices are amazing, given the expense of baking diabetic goods, ranging as little as $5-$8 a pound. Cheaper still are some of the pre-packaged gift boxes at the front of the store for under $5. **Hours:** 9:30am-5:30pm, Mon-Sat, Closed Sun. **Bus Line:** 201*.

The Candy Factory

4790 S. Eastern Avenue at Tropicana Avenue (458-1777) – A fun, relatively new store that offers everything you need to make your own candies: ingredients, sprinkles, molds, fillings and even a free introductory candy making class! The manager is a pleasant woman named Barbara who offers a little tour of the store, so take advantage of it. There are some fun things to see, and she is more than generous when offering samples of some of her home baked goods. There are also sugar-free candies like English toffee and caramel chews ($1.25) that are also low in fat (and they don't taste like rubber cement). She also sells bark candy (thin pan chunks) that come in wonderful flavors from strawberry to mint. The prices, especially when you buy them by high volume, rounds out to less than $5 a pound. **Hours:** 10am-6pm, Mon-Sat, 10am-5pm, Sun. **Bus Lines:** 110, 201*.

Mrs. Williams Diabetic Delights

3466 S. Decatur Boulevard at Spring Mountain Road (362-1243) – The diabetics delight for those on the westside of town. It's a small store but the nice variety of candies, cookies, cheesecakes, pies, muffins, syrups, cake mixes and ice cream only scratches the surface of its incredible variety of sugar-free products. Remember that the cost to make fine and tasty sugar-free sweets is considerably higher than regular candies. A pound of Williams' diabetic delights will cost you approximately $10.50, but there are some prepackaged and selected gift items that are cheaper. They have loads of samples you can try, I suggest you taste their English toffee, or raspberry delights. There's even a list that breaks down all the products into carbohydrates, calories, fat protein and cholesterol. For top-notch diabetic baked goods, Mrs. Williams shoots and scores. **Hours:** 10am-5:30, Mon-Sat, Closed Sun. **Bus Lines:** 103, 203.

Diamond Bakery

4255 Spring Mountain Road, C-110 inside Chinatown Plaza (368-1886) – Just one peek through the window and you'll see a whole bunch of goodies. Green and red paste cookies, egg white rolls with poppy-seed and coconut ($2 a bag) and a variety of bun snacks like onion and egg roll, hot dog in a yellow bun, shredded BBQ pork, or chicken in a bun ($0.85). The cakes are the true wonder. I implore you to try their key lime, or strawberry & pineapple mousse cake topped with sugar fruit slices ($1.35 a piece) – they're delicious. **Hours:** 9am-9pm, daily. **Bus Line:** 203.

DBA Snack House

4255 Spring Mountain Road, #C-104 at Wynn Road (247-9688) – An agreeable place to stop if you've just had a heavy meal at any number of the fine restaurants at the Chinatown Plaza. Although this shop is literally lined with wall-to-wall snacks like plums, mangos, candies, and a huge, intriguing variety of sweet and sours, make a point to have one of the tropical drinks. The Passion Fruit Jelly with Tapioca, Passion Fruit Green Tea with Jelly ($2.75), the delicious Cappuccino with Tapioca, or Coconut juice ($2.50) are satisfying ways to end a long day. **Hours:** 11am-9pm, daily. **Bus Line:** 203.

Weber Thrift Shop

3601 Rancho Drive at Gowan Road (658-4202) – If you are heading north on Rancho on your way to I-95 toward Mt. Charleston, you may want to stop here. Located just north of Cheyenne Avenue, Weber sells a whole lot of snacking goods for just pocket change. Now, a lot of Weber's products are sugary-sweet items like zingers, hostess cupcakes, and twinkies (under 40¢), but a good deal of them are also bread products like a single loaf of Cracked Wheat, Dutch Dill Rye, or Parisian Sourdough for only a $1. Dinner rolls, cereal bars, and liters of soda are also available. Granted, your picnic basket should be stocked before you leave on a road trip. Still, it never hurts to know about a place like this since it is not too far out of the way to your destination. **Hours:** 9am-6pm, Mon-Sat, 10am-5pm, Sun. **Bus Line**: 106, 218 (these buses run only once an hour).

Flomar Bakery

1083 E. Tropicana Avenue at Maryland Parkway (736-4306) – If you're near the university and need a sweet fix, skip the unsatisfying "desserts" at any of the numerous fast food chains that abound around there and try this bakery. Flomar may not have much, but this old bakery (est. 1976, remember, that's old for a small business in Las Vegas) has a selection of cakes and donuts that are deliciously addictive *and* cheap. *Please* try the ameretto cake, cheesecakes, or the coconut cream white cake, and if you're lucky, they might have their house specialty, Chocolate Kulua Cake (all just $1.25 for a big two-layer slice). One taste of these and that McFlurry's from MacDonalds, or that paltry sliver of a cheesecake at Carl's Jr. won't quite seem the same. They have good donuts and cookies too (40-60¢). **Hours:** 8am-6pm, Mon-Sat, 2pm-5pm, Sun. **Bus Lines:** 109*, 201*.

Chapter 6

Cool Cafes and Pubthumbing

As in all major cities, cafes in Vegas are the spots where you can meet students, artists, and other alternative cultural wannabes. Pubs are where you go to for casual conversation after work, and Cafes, well — I'll leave that to your agenda. Vegas is actually a nice surprise in that we have a good variety for both of the above, and it's all pretty affordable, providing you curb your excesses. Fortunately, the ones I felt worth mentioning in this book are located in the central part of town, making them easily attainable for travelers.

Cafe's

Liquid Culture Cafe Espresso Roma

4400 Maryland Parkway at Harmon Avenue (369-1540) — Cafe Roma, located directly across from the University (UNLV), has been a popular stop for students for years. In fact, it was one of the first in the city. So laid back it's supine, this cafe is populated with thinkers, slackers and administrators. There are plenty of magazines scattered around the cafe with subject matter ranging from analyzing Goethe to gay gossip. There's an event calendar on the wall that lists the latest music gigs, poetry recitals and film festivals in town. The décor is typical of an "off-the-cuff" collegiate hangout: marble tables with uneven legs, a variety of sofas in different colors, and a cracked floor with hand dripped paint. Occasionally, they have music performances, but the real fascination lies with their open mike poetry reading contest. From the excruciatingly pretentious to the giddily amateurish, Las Vegas poets are never without their entertainment value. You can catch them on Monday nights, at 8pm. **Hours:** 7am-Midnight, Sun-Thurs, 8am-Midnight, Fri-Sat. **Best House Item** — The croissants, namely the raspberry, with real fruit inside laced with light frosting on top — tasty and only $1.85. The Brain, a mixture of four shots of espresso with whipped cream and honey, and the Roma Turtle, a combination of mocha, English toffee, and walnut syrup ($3.90) gets raves too. **Bus Lines:** 109*, 213.

Cafe Copioh

4500 Maryland Parkway at Harmon Avenue (739-0305) — Another popular stop for students is this cafe, which is also located directly across from UNLV. Copioh has done a solid job in creating one of the most relaxing and student-friendly atmospheres you'll find in Las Vegas. From one-joke board games like Anti-Monopoly, to the tattered pea-green sofa with missing legs and lumpy cushions, there's an air of true collegiate freshness. Best of all are Copioh's fascinating "guest speakers". Among my favorites over the years have been former residents of Roswell, retelling stories of military conspiracy with all the giddy paranoia of an "X-Files" fanatic, and a dominatrix teaching you the tricks of her trade. Half-baked (but sometimes pointed) poetry readings, Student Theater, palm reading and other assortments of low-brow fun seeking abound in this place. Sure it may sound a little flaky, but the atmosphere here is anything but listless. When you have good cappuccino, interesting conversation and colorful entertainment, it's a tough combination to beat. **Hours**: 3pm-12:30am, Sun-Thurs, 3pm-1am, Fri, 3pm-1:30am, Sat. **Best House Item** – The Deception ($3), sort of like a mocha slush with peanut butter, with an added touch of raspberry syrup. **Bus Lines:** 109*, 213.

Enigma Garden Café

918 S. 4th Street north of Charleston Boulevard (386-0999) – Located just a block west from the strip, this outdoor cafe has a relaxing, grass-roots feel to it. One of the owners, Lenadams Dorris, is a radio host for a local station, and pops up on TV now and then as a popular horticulturist, so it's one of those in-the-know places. Since he's a Mr. Green Thumb, Len made the vegetation in this place wild. In the summer, you'd swear you were slashing through the Brazilian rain forest with thick plants, vines, long stemmed fur trees, and the like. It's the usual fare on the menu: bagels, pastries, sandwiches, cappuccino, espresso and some specialty drinks (Italian sodas, mochas, blended fruit drinks) but they're all under $3. There's a small theater at the Enigma and up and coming young bands will try to break in their sound to a very receptive audience. They also have open-mike poetry reading, and if you read my review of Cafe Espresso's gigs, then you'll get the idea for this one too. Best of all, for a few months of the year (normally May-September) this place is opened 24 hours, making it an intoxicating outdoor setting for you to experience Las Vegas in the pre-dawn hours, and it's only minutes away from the strip. One of the great "hanging" spots in Vegas. **Hours:** It varies, so call ahead, but it's normally 7am-10pm. **Best House Item:** Food – Bombay Chicken Salad. A filling, heavenly concoction with a Cuban chicken breast and vegetables in a creamy curried sweet and sour dressing, served on greens with carrots peppers and bananas ($5.95). Drink – Bananarama, a bit of seltzer, cream, banana and Swiss chocolate ($2). **Bus Line:** 206*.

Fritters Café & Deli

316 Bridger Avenue west of 4th Street (384-3115) – Both affordable and comfortable, this place ranks a notch above other cafés in the downtown area. Everything is decorated in calming hues of blue, (dark, sea, baby, sky blue, etc.) from the tables and napkins, to the walls and plates. The sandwiches are a must with the two best being the Stanley Steamer (pastrami and Swiss cheese steamed to a heavenly melt on your choice of a kaiser roll or rye), or the Vegetarian Vegetarian (cream cheese spread, sprouts, avocado, mozzarella, Swiss, tomato, on nut bread), which are served with potato salad ($4.60). Soups, breakfast bagels, and muffins as well as any kind of espresso, cappuccino, or Italian sodas are also served ($1.60). **Hours:** 7:30-4:45 pm, Mon-Fri., closed on the weekends. **Best House Item:** It's a tough call between the Stanley Steamer and the Vegetarian Vegetarian, but I'll go with the veggie. It's just slightly different from the norm and I'm a sucker for cream cheese with *anything*. **Bus Line:** 207.

Danube Café

4685 S. Pecos Road at Tropicana Avenue (454-5535) – A favorite spot whenever I'm on the eastside of town. Laid back and casual, they serve salads, falafels, gyros, goulash, sandwiches, and assorted espresso drinks. There's also a mini-market where you can buy Persian themed knick-knacks (breadbaskets, small rugs, clocks) and coffee beans of many flavorings. The owner comes from Los Angeles, and he must have been pretty popular there because there are scores of autographed pictures of celebrities (you gotta have Stallone) that stud the walls. Try their daily lunch specials that change, of course, from day to day, which can be anything from Greek styled Roasted Pork and potatoes served with salad, to Pork Chops with vegetables and parsley potatoes ($6.95). **Hours:** 10-8 pm, Mon-Fri. 10-5 pm Sat, Closed Sun. **Best House Item:** They offer a generous portion of Mousaka, a delicious eggplant meal topped with ground beef and Parmesan sauce ($5.95). **Bus Lines:** 111, 201*.

Pubs & Bars

Crown and Anchor Pub

Tropicana Avenue east of Maryland Parkway (739-8676) – This British styled pub has long been a favorite for both UNLV students and professors. It's hard *not* to understand why. The variety of beer is great. ESB lager, Woodpecker cider, and Guinness are just some of the imports. Their dinners are distinctly English with anything from Shepherd's pie to fish and chips (both $6.95). If you really like this kind of food, your best bet is to come on Mondays. That's when they have the all-you-can-eat (if you haven't guessed by now, the all-you-can-stomach concept is a mainstay of food specials in this town) fish and chips; they spare no quarter in the portions ($8). Anglophiles will also appreciate the best English desserts in town. Both the Sherried Trifle (sponge cake, raspberries, custard doused with sherry and topped with fresh cream) and the English Apple Custard (hot apple cobbler with crumb topping served with fresh custard, both $3.25) are often ordered and praised. The most enjoyable aspect about this pub is that it acts like a magnet to all the Britons of the city, since they carry much-missed ales from back home. The jukebox plays like a retro of your favorite '80s Britpop (i.e. The Police, Squeeze, UB40 – you get the picture). You'll be served by genuine English waitresses, can indulge in dart playing, and read interesting U.S. based publications for Brits, the most noteworthy being "Union Jack". This paper has an amazing collection of advertisements for travel agencies that specialize in discount travel to Europe. This is a fun and snazzy place – drop in. **Hours:** 11am-6am, daily. **Bus Lines:** 109*, 201*.

The Dispensary Lounge

2451 E. Tropicana Avenue at Eastern Avenue (458-6343) – This joint is a leftover from the '70s, but it's nevertheless fascinating in its adamant refusal to swing with the times. Let me describe the décor: a water wheel is spinning on the far wall from the entrance, living room furniture is scattered in the middle of the bar, makeshift tables are topped with candles, and '70s memorabilia is sloppily tacked onto the walls. One can almost hear the wah-wah guitar effects from a bad Elliott Gould movie. Strange as it seems, the disarming bad taste of this bar gets more accommodating with every beer. There's a good-natured looseness to the place that I really enjoy. Even better are the reasonably priced drafts. Domestics are a mere $1.50 while imports are just a dollar more. Bottles are also inexpensive with imports never being more than $3. If you're interested, their St. Patrick Day celebrations are the best in town, with green-dyed beer and free appetizers. **Hours:** 24 hours, daily. **Bus Lines:** 110, 201*.

Boston Bar and Grill

3417 S. Jones at Spring Mountain Road (368-0760) – Don't be misled by their name. This is no ordinary bar and grill, but one of the prime spots in town for nurturing excellent local bands. Boston Bar and Grill (just call it "The Boston", those in the know do) has received such good press lately that they've managed to attract bands from all over the southwest (Phoenix, Los Angeles, Tucson, Las Vegas, etc.). It's not terribly roomy and the acoustics can be a bit thick, but the energy and enthusiasm of the crowd and the musical virtuosity and stamina of the bands *more* than compensates for the slight drawbacks. Throw in good grub and drink specials from the bar and you've got yourself a hanging spot. **Hours:** 24 hours, daily. **Bus Lines:** 102, 203.

Legends Lounge

865 N. Lamb Boulevard at Washington Avenue (437-9674), www.tapetree.com/legends — Legends Lounge not only has a strong reputation with local writers, but "Rolling Stone" magazine named Legends as one of the city's top music venues. A terrific sound system, genial staff who appreciate loyal customers, and fine pop-rock bands — together create a very inviting ambience. Legends Lounge is head and shoulders above all others when it comes to supporting local bands (only the Boston can *try* to rival them in this regard). Local groups play here almost every night. Legends also features many up and coming bands from all across the country as well – that's right, the acoustics and reception are *that* good. It's not an easy place to get to, but if you like good music, then Legends is the vibe you're looking for – check out their website for scheduled gigs. **Hours:** 24 hours, daily. **Bus Line:** 112.

Holy Cow Casino Café & Brewery

2423 Las Vegas Boulevard South at Sahara Avenue (732-2697) – I *love* this place. It's so endearingly tacky, knowing just what its customers want in terms of trappings. Their microbrewery has some terrific deals during happy hour ($1 drafts). There's also a string of gaudy collectibles like moo-clocks and cow creamers. Even if it's something you don't care to own, you have to admire the imagination that goes into all these cow-theme products. A definite plus about the Holy Cow is that the clientele is more friendly than other watering holes on the strip. **Hours:** It's on the strip so of course it's 24 hours every day. **Bus Lines:** 204, 301*, 302*.

Moose McGillycuddy's

4770 S. Maryland Parkway south of Harmon Avenue (798-8337) – One of the most popular student hangouts in town and located directly across from the University. Cheap beer, dancing until 4am in the morning, live bands and DJ's all add up to a pretty hip collective. Saturday nights are busy, but it might be worth it to take advantage of the 50% off drinks and appetizers between 4pm-9pm. Wednesday night is also popular due to $1 drafts and $2 imported bottled beer specials. Moose's food specials vary from time to time, but they always have something going on and the youthful bounce of the crowd seldom slows down. **Hours:** 11am-2am, Mon-Fri, 11am-4am, Fri-Sat. **Bus Lines:** 109*, 201*.

Sand Dollar Blues Lounge

3335 W. Spring Mountain Road at Polaris Street (871-6651), www.blueslasvegas.com – A small bar that is big on vibe, music, and liquor. You can count on a live band playing a cool selection of blues, swing and jazz every night – no other bar in Las Vegas has such credentials. The friendly atmosphere of barflies and aging musicians only adds to the fun. Only the unpretentious are welcomed. **Hours:** 24 hours, daily. **Bus Line:** 203.

Mad Dog's and Englishmen

515 Las Vegas Boulevard South at Bonneville Avenue (382-5075) – A fine pub with good fish-n-chips, the always reliable Guiness and Blackthorn on tap and a few people fiddling around the jukebox wondering which Kinks song to play. Some prefer our city's other English pub, the Crown and Anchor, which is a little more collegiate and energetic; but to most of us locals, Mad Dog's serves two important services for a pub – good grub and beer! Better still, it's right on the Boulevard, so you have access to a good night-cap if you're downtown. Your best bet is to drop in during the weekdays between 4pm-6pm, that's when you'll get ½ price appetizers and $1 drafts. **Hours**: 24 hours, daily. **Bus Line**: 301*.

Double Down Saloon

4640 Paradise Road off Harmon Avenue (791-5775) – A local paper once described this dive as "the best place to avoid yuppie scum." Do you want the ultimate in unpretentiousness? Then the Double Down is for you. This joint has cheap beer, pool tables with sun-dried covers and found-it-in-the-dumpster couches. A definite plus for DD is the best jukebox of any bar that I've ever experienced. Anything from ska, punk, swing, power pop, doo-wop, southern rock, and jazz can be played for a few quarters. **Hours**: 24 hours, daily. **Bus Line**: 108.

Champagnes Café

3557 S. Maryland Parkway at Twain Avenue (737-1699) – With its gaudy red velvet wallpaper, wall of cigarette smoke, leather couches, cheap beer and quirky denizens, Champagnes Café comes across as one the most delightfully tacky bars you'll ever see. Sure, it might be overdoing it with the numerous photos of pop iconoclasts (Jimmy Dean and Marilyn posters) and the limited jukebox selection doesn't exactly have people dancing over to it with abandon, but the vibe in this place is so strangely and terrifically welcoming that you won't be distracted by these shortcomings. **Bus Lines:** 109*, 213.

Huntridge Tavern

1122 E. Charleston Boulevard at Maryland Parkway (384-7377) – The Huntridge Tavern is pure minimalism: little décor, dim lighting and no discount margarita specials, just good, ol'-fashioned drinks, served quickly and inexpensively. If you've just caught a show at the Huntridge Theater (which is just across the street), head toward the Tavern. The low-key, unassuming atmosphere here makes it a great place to unwind. **Bus Lines:** 109*, 206*.

Triple Play

1875 S. Decatur Boulevard at Oakey Boulevard (364-0808) – Triple Play may seem like your average neighborhood bar — with big screen television sets so you can watch the latest baseball games and a few denizens at the bar playing video poker as they chain smoke the night away. But amidst this unassuming atmosphere lies one magnificent exception – its Philly Steak and Cheese sandwich. They *pile* on the tender sirloin tip and cram it with fried onions, sauteed mushrooms, green peppers and Swiss cheese and *somehow* manage to shove it into a 12" loaf ($5.75). This is one of those sandwiches where you request a fork so you can eat the rest of the beef that has spilled onto your plate. **Hours:** 24 hours, daily. **Bus Lines:** 103. 205.

Four Kegs

276 N. Jones Boulevard south of Washington Boulevard (870-0255) – This author's favorite neighborhood bar has been offering what locals have known for almost 20 years – the best Stramboli sandwiches in town. The small one alone is mighty filling. It's 8" long and you get your choice of veggie, turkey & Swiss, beef & cheddar, or the "original" (all $5.25). The 13" large is $8.25. From midnight to 11 am, the Stramboli's are only ½ price! Also during this time try the Sicilian pizza, it's also half price and at $3.50 (regular size with six pieces) a great value. The beer variety isn't overwhelming (standards like Coors, Shinerbock, Budweiser and Killian's Red), but at $1.50 a draught, it certainly won't break you. The atmosphere is just what you want in a small bar: friendly, easy conversation with other barflies and the bartender. Only the cocktail drinks don't make the grade. The strawberry daiquiris and margaritas are only a little stronger than the fresh fruit slush at your local Stop n' Go, but that's nitpicking in an otherwise fine neighborhood bar. **Hours:** 24 hours, daily. **Bus Line:** 102.

Pogo's Tavern

2103 N. Decatur Boulevard off Lake Mead Boulevard (646- 9735) – One the great assets of having friends who are musicians is their ability to open me up to new vistas in this city that I think I know so well, and to renew my zeal for discovery in the process. Until recently, I was unaware of

Pogo's Tavern; a small, cinder-block structure that's been around for over 30 years. "It's not just the cheap drinks and the twenty five cent game of pool that attracts me here," said a clarinetist friend of mine. "It's also the great jazz musicians that jam here every Friday night!" True to his word, every Friday, from 8pm to Midnight, a group of old-timers gather on stage (such as it is) and start playing Jazz. What I like best about Pogo's is the inviting atmosphere. It's not uncommon to see other musicians get caught up in the mood and join the band onstage. Even if you're not a lover of Jazz, this is one neighborhood bar where pleasant conversation and a relaxing vibe are easily available to anyone that walks through the door. It's a real delight (I just wish they'd fix that flickering light bulb in the old Budweiser sign – but wait, perhaps that's part of the charm?). **Bus Lines**: 103, 210.

Chapter 7

Malls and Flea Markets

Malls tend to look alike, no matter which part of the country you live in. Las Vegas is no exception, but as a courtesy, and if you're the kind of person that loves to people-watch in that singular American experience – mall culture – then it's only fair that I list what we have here. The flea markets are much more varied and interesting, with the added bonus of finding some terrific deals on eccentric items, ranging from Asian incense sticks to discount militia clothing. If you want to make a day of mall hopping, take bus 402. It's our city's only cross-town bus, and it serves almost all of the city's major malls. All other major shopping outlets can be easily accessed by the city's other bus lines.

The Fashion Show Mall

3200 Las Vegas Boulevard South at Spring Mountain Road (369-8382) – A standard mall located on the strip across from the Desert Inn. It's very popular with tourists, and thus usually crowded. The two-story building contains over 145 shops: Saks Fifth Avenue, Neiman Marcus, Bullocks's, etc. The food court has all the junk food you're familiar with: Hot Dogs on a Stick, Dairy Queen frozen treats, Cinnabon, etc. **Hours:** 10am-9pm, Mon-Fri, 10am-7pm, Sat, Noon-6pm, Sun. **Bus Lines:** 203, 301*, 302*.

Belz Factory Outlet World

7400 Las Vegas Boulevard South (896-5599), www.belz.com – A tremendously huge discount mall, claimed to be the largest factory outlet mall in the country. You can save a bundle on major brand names like Levi's, Geoffrey Bean, Cornell Kitchenware, and the like. If you're here in the month of January (the after Christmas sale), definitely stop by, these stores will mark down their merchandize by as much as 75%. The selection is enormous, with over 145 stores to choose from that deal with merchandise directly from the manufacturer. There are several information booths if you have any questions, and there's a food court with everything from burritos, yogurt shops, pizza, and that staple of all mall food fare – Baskin-Robbins Ice Cream. As for the shops, they include The Casio Factory Outlet – A large selection of Casio keyboards, watches, stereos, portable TV's, daily organizers and more, available at rock bottom prices. Casio Factory also carries a wide selection of other brand names like JVC, Minolta, Maxell, and many more.

Another store to seek out is Ultra Jewelers – An eclectic selection of fine jewelry, pennants, rings, bracelets, charms, and watches, and other assorted closeouts from the manufacturer. You make out like a bandit with sales up to 75% off. **Hours:** 10am-9pm, Mon-Sat, 10am-6pm, Sun. **Bus Lines:** 112, 303.

Las Vegas Factory Stores

9155 Las Vegas Boulevard South (897-9090) – Located about five miles further south on the strip than the Belz Factory Outlet, this is a great place for the bargain hunter, but the merchandise is more on the low-end than Belz Factory. Discount perfume, CDs, books, clothes, and souvenirs are just some of the items you can buy. One word of caution – this is an outdoor mall. In the summer, when the mercury hits 116F, there isn't so much as a mist system to keep you cool. However, you might think it's worth the journey when you consider that you can save between 30%-70% off retail price on virtually anything. **Hours:** 10am-7pm, Mon-Sat, 10am-6pm, Sun. **Bus Line:** 303.

The Meadows Mall

4300 Meadows Lane (878-4849), www.themeadowsmall.com – A neighborhood mall, and therefore more "teen" oriented than the others. There are 144 stores to choose from including the big department stores like Sears, Penny's, Dillards, and Broadway. There is a food court with the usual delights ranging from burgers and pizzas to gyros. **Hours:** 10am-9pm, Mon-Fri, 10am-7pm, Sat, 10am-6pm, Sun. **Bus Lines:** 103, 104, 207, 402.

The Boulevard Mall

3528 Maryland Parkway at Desert Inn Road (735-8268) – The locals' favorite mall. For some reason, the food, the variety of the stores, and the atmosphere are just what we like. This mall has less tourist-oriented paraphernalia than the others and more practical services like hair salons, travel agencies, automotive repair, and those ever popular one-hour photo processing shops. It's handy for tourists since there is an exchange rate vending machine for foreign currency that'll give you a fair exchange rate. Sears, JC Penny, Dillards and other stores that are staples of mall culture are located here. The Boulevard is generally considered to have one of the best food courts in town. Vegetarian entrees, Fruit Blends, Teriyaki Bowls, and an excellent Mexican grill are just some of the above-average (for a suburban shopping mall) grub you can get. It's a convenient stop for visitors, and only a 10-15 minute drive from the strip, depending on the traffic. There are three covered parking garages and free valet parking, and the bus service is frequent, so accessibility is never a problem. **Hours:** 10am–9pm, Mon-Fri, 10am-8pm, Sat, 11am-6pm, Sun. **Bus Lines:** 109*, 213.

Galleria at Sunset Mall

1300 Sunset Road at Stephanie Street (434-0202), www.galleriaatsunset.com – One of the newer malls in town, located in Green Valley, a suburban town development which is really Henderson, Nevada. It's located right across the street from the Sunset Station Hotel & Casino – Henderson's most popular casino. There are over 130 stores (including the big hitters: Macys, Dillards, Sears, etc.) in this two-story mall, and yes, it has a food court loaded with junk foods. **Hours:** 10am-9 pm, Mon-Sat, 11am-6pm, Sun. **Bus Lines:** 112, 117, 402.

Broadacres Outdoor Swap Meet

2930 Las Vegas Boulevard North at Pecos Road (642-3777) – Talk about unexpected delights! I've been to many swap meets in my time, but few could match the surprising level of zaniness that Broadacres offers. There's a carnival-like atmosphere to this swap meet, and, if you're lucky, you might even catch a barker who will lead you to something "mysterious" in the middle of the premises. It's practically like a big rummage sale, since locals, or anyone else, can pay the minimum $13 fee for use of an 8'x10' space and sell whatever merchandise they want (excluding hardcore porno). Therefore, it's difficult to predict which established businesses will be selling on any given day. All the same, if you're looking for good values, they have them here. There are cheap, brand name luggage sets like Transworld and Samsonite, discounted fruit and vegetable stands, toys for a dollar and under, comic books, and a huge selection of power tools for wickedly cheap prices. Since this is one of the biggest shopping centers in the city that caters to Latinos, salespeople of produce stores and record shops, and even some real estate agents (that's right, you can buy parcels of land here) speak only in Spanish. One of the key pleasures about Broadacres is the food. You'll find everything from a 1/3 lb. hamburger smothered in French dressing and Bermuda onions cooked for you on an open flamed grill, to taco shops, teriyaki bowls, Chinese take-out, hot dog vendors and an ice cream truck that drives around the lot. All in all, if you're the type that loves to hunt for cool, unpredictable stuff, then call this place home. **One word of caution.** Beware of purchasing big electrical merchandise (i.e., CD players, televisions, VCR's) from some of the merchants. They have a reputation for poor return policies, so if anything should go wrong with an item purchased (frequent visitors have told me this is often the case), you're pretty much out of luck. **Hours:** 6:30pm-

8pm, Fri-Sun. **Admission:** Friday - $0.50, Sat.-Sun., $1, Children under 11 with an adult get in for free. **Bus Lines:** 111, 113*.

Fantastic Indoor Swap Meet

1717 S. Decatur Boulevard at Oakey Boulevard (877-0087), www.fantasticswap.com – The entrance fee is only a dollar to what is advertised as Nevada's largest swap meet. Here you'll find a variety of goods, and unlike Broadacres Outdoor Swap Meet (listed above), the stores at Fantastic tend to be more established. You'll gain a consistency of merchants here, but you'll lose the freewheeling, unpredictable charm of Broadacres. The interior is slim, with only wafer-thin barriers that divide the merchants into their territories, adding the frustration of constantly tripping over the not-so-well-laid lime-green carpeting. Still, with over 200 stores, it would be hard not to find something you like. The variety is good, with discount watches and jewelry, herbal bath products, cutlery, gourmet coffee grounds, women's lingerie, discount videos, African jewelry, cheap sunglasses, and the list goes on and on. Since the merchants are here on a permanent basis, you can check the website to see who's in and who's out. The food is nothing to sing about, but there's a hot dog stand and a donut shop, just in case you get hungry. **Hours:** 10am-6pm, Fri-Sun. **Bus Lines:** 103, 205.

Antique Warehouse

4175 S. Cameron, #1 at Flamingo Road (251-3447) – This is Nevada's largest antique store and their inventory includes toys, dolls, furniture, collectibles, music and gifts, along with a stunning collection of rare autographs. It's a big store and you're encouraged to roam around the place. It can be a little pricey, and unless you have a strong head for knowing your stuff and appraising the antiques, you'll have little chance to work down the price tag. **Hours:** 10am-5pm, Mon-Sat, 11am-4pm, Sun. **Bus Lines:** 104, 202*.

The Forum Shops at Caesar's Palace

3500 Las Vegas Boulevard South (893-4800), www.shopcaesars.com – This is the Caesars' famed shopping villa that transports you back to ancient Rome, complete with statues, hand-painted skies on a dome-shaped ceiling, huge fountains, and buff, male models dressed in ancient garb reminiscent of "Caliguila." Everyone loves the show "Atlantis," which runs every hour on the hour for 10 minutes, between 11-10pm. Over 50,000 gallons of water is used in this aquarium show, complete with holograms, fire, and amazing robotic statues that move with a surprising suppleness. As for the stores – well, they're pretty costly. It's essentially window-shopping for the budget traveler although some stores will offer a good sale, so it never hurts to keep your eyes open. All in all, the atmosphere and showmanship of the Forum shops offers one of the neatest treats for free on the strip. **Hours:** 10am-11pm, Sun-Thurs, 10am-Midnight, Fri-Sat. **Bus Lines:** 202*, 301*, 302*.

The Tower Shops at Stratosphere

2000 Las Vegas Boulevard South (388-1130), www.stratlv.com – The poor man's Forum Shops, located on the second floor of the Stratosphere Tower. There's something so Vegas about a mall that welcomes you with a cheap reconstruction of the Eiffel Tower! Give these guys credit for making the most of their limited surroundings. For starters, there are the faux gas streetlights that designate the "avenues" in the mall, and a painted sky on the ceiling that is supposed to represent Paris on a spring afternoon (I won't describe this, you'll have to see it for yourself). Want more pseudo-cultural sophistication? Little replicas of New York and the lantern streets of Hong Kong will be discovered as you walk further down the hallway. With over 35 stores and 13 retail carts to choose from, this is a wise opportunity to buy a lot of standard Las Vegas belongings (cards, T-shirts, baseball caps, and dice clocks – for zanier products don't forget Bonanza Gift Shop up the road) at a cheap price. Plenty of restaurants and some neat little theme stores like magic shops and discounted perfume outlets only add to the unconventional appeal of this mall. **Hours:** 10am-11pm, Sun-Thurs, 10am-Midnight, Fri-Sat. **Bus Lines:** 108, 301*, 302*.

Chapter 8

Cheap Fun on the Strip and Downtown

Most of the headlining shows on the strip can run pretty high in cost. Vegas stalwarts Sigfried and Roy, who perform at the Mirage, are now $95 a show. The price doesn't drop off that much for Cirque Du Soleil at the Bellagio or a top theatrical production like EFX at MGM. Having seen all of these shows, I can tell you that while they were truly enthralling spectacles, I felt lucky to have received complimentary tickets because I just couldn't justify paying those prices.

There are many entertaining live shows to enjoy on both the strip and downtown that won't cost you too much. They range from the campy (but always entertaining) female impersonations, to Circus acts and comedy clubs. Aren't we diverse? Here's a brief rundown:

Shows

Viva Las Vegas at the Stratosphere Tower

2000 Las Vegas Boulevard South (380-7711), www.stratlv.com – The Rodney Dangerfield of all Las Vegas variety shows. "Viva Las Vegas" has trouble getting respect, and it's not entirely undeserved. It's an offbeat affair, but for only $11, it's not bad either. Like the plucky charm of those old Mickey Rooney and Judy Garland musicals from the 1940s, the sheer determination and good humor of the cast makes up for a lack of imagination and less than extravagant production values. This 90-minute review is complete with ventriloquists (I've always envied their talent), good singers, a charming set of dancers and a whimsical Welsh comic named Dave Swan. The only low-point comes when Swan does a painfully misguided parody of Elvis during his bloated Vegas years. It's the best variety show in Las Vegas for under $15 – if that's progress. *Important note* – if you're in the stratosphere tower and happen to be playing the slots, walk over to the bar just outside the theater. They occasionally offer a coupon that admits one for the price of a drink. **Admission**: $13.45, (including tax and gratuity), an adult must accompany anyone under 21 (but it's hardly adult material). **Showtimes**: 2pm & 4pm, Mon-Sat. **Bus Lines**: 108, 301*, 302*.

An Evening at La Cage at the Rivieva Hotel and Casino

2901 Las Vegas Boulevard South (794-9433), www.theriviera.com – Frank Marino has been playing in Las Vegas for over a decade and you won't find a better female impersonator in the city. Marino does an excellent incarnation as Joan Rivers and his boy-lesque troop do raucous takes on Tina Turner, Liza Minnelli, Diana Ross and Madonna. Kerr is a skilled monologist with crack Broadway timing and delivery and he's a trooper who rarely puts on a bad show. **Admission:** $33.58 (including tax, gratuity and one drink). **Showtimes:** 7:30pm & 9:30pm, Wed.-Mon. **Bus Lines:** 301*, 302.

Forever Plaid at the Flamingo Las Vegas

3555 Las Vegas Boulevard South (733-3333), www.lv-flamingo.com – This was the first Broadway show to come to Las Vegas (okay, officially off-Broadway). It's also a very underrated value for a good show on the strip. The premise is simple enough: a quartet of white bread harmony singers – The Plaids (named after their retro dinner jackets) – are killed in a car accident in 1964 when they have a head-on collision with a bus carrying a load of Beatles' fans. They return to earth in the form of blithe spirits to play their dream gig – a Las Vegas Club date! Among the strengths of this show are the fine orchestra, a versatile selection of songs from doo-wop to swing, to a terrific of calypso with Harry Belefonte's "The Banana Boat Song," and four strong vocal leads who harmonize well together. The sight gags and jokes might be corny, but they're delivered with a verve and freshness that never makes the material stale. The brisk pacing (it's a 90 minute show but it felt like 45 minutes to me) never lets the bittersweet theatrics seem cloying. **Admission:** $27.44 (including tax and gratuity). **Showtimes:** 7:30pm & 10pm, Tue-Sat. **Bus Lines:** 202*, 301*, 302*.

Les Trix at the San Remo Hotel

115 E. Tropicana Avenue at Koval Lane (597-6028), www.sanremolasvegas.com — A trio of beautiful, scantily clad (in the later show they're topless) young ladies sing, dance and perform magic tricks to a captivating effect. The showroom is somewhat small, seating only 180 people, but given the robust attributes of the performers, the snug confines work very well. Comedian Joe Trammel acts as a comic MC and the whole show has a sly, cheerful air that the audience definitely appreciates. **Admission:** $31.50 (including tax, gratuity and one drink). **Showtimes:** 8pm & 10:30 pm daily, Tue-Sun, because the 10:30 p.m. performance is topless, no one under 21 will be admitted. **Bus Lines:** 201*, 213, 301*, 302*.

Rides & Galleries

Eiffel Tower Ride at the Paris Hotel

3655 Las Vegas Boulevard South (946-7000), www.paris-lv.com – I'll leave it to you to pass judgement on this ride. Personally, I found it a bit disappointing. Sure, the view of the strip from 370 feet above ground is impressive. Especially at night, where the busy designs of all the neon lights blend leisurely into a seamless stream (avoid the daytime, unless you're dying to see what subdivision housing or road construction in our valley looks like). However, there are drawbacks. First you have a *very* long wait in front of you, anywhere from 30-50 minutes because the elevator capacity is small. It fits ten people at best, so the line chisels away ever so slowly until it's your turn. There are no restrooms in the Eiffel Tower or on the lobby floor, which is located a level above the casino floor, so those of you with small bladders have been forewarned. Once you get to the top, you'll pretty much be walking with your elbows caved into your abdomen because the Circular walkway at the top is claustrophobically narrow. Add the inconvenience that you have to wait in line to go *back* down the elevator (there's no limit as to how long you can stay at the observation deck – hence the overcrowding) makes it less than prime fun. Still, for some visitors, the view is worth it. **Hours:** 9am-1am, daily. **Admission:** $8, children and seniors (65 and over) is $6. **Bus Lines:** 202*, 301*, 302*.

Merlin's Magic Motion Rides at the Excalibur Hotel

3850 Las Vegas Boulevard South (597-7777), www.excaliburcasino.com – Two unique, 48-seat facilities that show an impressive film experience. Although you sit down and never leave the theater, you feel like you're being taken on a wild ride, as ear-splitting sound and 70 mm visual effects surround you in this three-minute, rollercoaster-like experience. **Hours:** 10am-12:45am, Mon-Fri, 9am-12:45 am, Sat-Sun. **Admission:** $4, free for children under 42". **Bus Lines:** 201*, 301*, 302*.

Tower & Thrill Rides at the Stratosphere

2000 Las Vegas Hotel South (380-7777), www.stratlv.com – The tallest free standing tower in America. Not only is it a breathtaking vantagepoint to view a panoramic sweep of the city (it's a staggering 1,149 feet above ground!), but it also houses two Thrill rides: the high roller (an unnerving swirl around the tower point) and the big shot (an exhilarating vertical shot in the air). They don't last for more than two minutes, but man, it's an adrenaline rush! **Admission**: Observation Tower – $6, Local Residents – $3, Children under 3 – Free. **Rides**: Big Shot – $6, High Roller – $5., **Hours**: 10am – 1am, Sun-Thurs; 10am-2am, Fri-Sat. **Bus Lines**: 108, 301*, 302*.

Manhattan Express Rollercoaster at New York New York

3790 Las Vegas Boulevard South (740-6969), www.nynyhotelcasino.com – Now here's a rollercoaster that, while it only lasts two minutes and is a little costly, is thrilling because you're practically dangling over the strip upside down. It has, they claim, the first ever heartline twist and dive maneuver, which is similar to the sensation felt by a pilot during a barrel roll in an airplane. For an additional $7, you can purchase pictures of your facial expressions, which are taken during the rollercoaster ride. **Hours**: 10am-11pm, daily. **Admission:** $10. **Bus Lines:** 201*, 301*, 302*.

Sahara Speedworld at the Sahara Hotel

2535 Las Vegas Boulevard South (737-2471), www.saharahotelandcasino.com – A virtual-reality, three-quarter scale, Indy car stimulated race. The 40,000 square foot facility features 24 interactive rides plus two 24-seat 3-D theaters. Fun, but overrun with screaming youngsters on the weekend. **Hours:** 10am-10pm, Sun-Thurs, 10am-11pm, Fri-Sat. **Admission:** Grand Prix Race (this is a lot more fun) – $8, 3-D Theater – $3. **Bus Lines:** 204, 301*, 302*.

Madame Tussaud's at the Venetian Resort

3355 Las Vegas Boulevard South (367-1847), www.venetian.com – You can have your picture taken with eerie wax replications of movie stars (Brad Pitt, Sean Connery), athletes (Arnold Palmer, Babe Ruth), and pop stars (Madonna, Jimi Hendrix). The most fun and distinct part of the tour are the replications that are a celebration of Las Vegas' past: Bugsy Siegel, Wolfgang Puck, Liberace and my favorite, an animatronic Elvis! Also interesting is the gallery that contains photos and videos of the meticulous detail that's involved in this unique artistry (i.e. the body measurements, how the skin and eyes are painted, how the hair strands are placed onto the head). **Admission:** $12.50, Local Resident's & Seniors – $10.75, Children under 12 – $10, Children under 3 – Free. **Hours:** 10am–10pm, daily. **Bus Lines:** 201*, 202*, 301*, 302*.

The Adventuredome at Circus Circus Hotel and Casino

2880 Las Vegas Boulevard South (794-3745), www.CircusCircus-lasvegas.com – A big, 5-acre theme park. Sort of campy, but certainly unique – even by Vegas standards. There are full-sized dinosaurs, cliff dwellings, 90-ft. waterfalls, and some fun rides. All the more interesting is that it's in a climate-controlled dome, so there's this eerie biosphere element to it. Features the only indoor, double-loop, double corkscrew roller coaster in the United States. **Hours:** Daily, 11-10 pm **Admission: $**15.95 for an all day pass. Otherwise, rides are between $2-$5. **Bus Lines:** 301*, 302*.

Star Trek: The Experience at Las Vegas Hilton

3000 Paradise Road off Karen Avenue (888–462-6539, 732-5111) – The ultimate utopia for all you trekkers out there. Since it's opening in the summer of 1997, fans of the television show from all over the world have visited this "experience." You'll become a starfleet member when you enter the room and embark on an intergalactic journey that utilizes simulator rides, interactive videos, virtual-reality stations, holograms, and state-of-the-art computer games. The "voyage" will begin in the disarmingly titled "history of the future museum," filled with authentic Star Trek costumes, weaponry, and props. From the Starfleet Gallery room, you'll be beamed up to the bridge of the Starship enterprise and board a shuttlecraft for a simulated journey through the universe. Here you'll travel through various galaxies and battle those ever-popular villains – the Klingons. Upon successful completion of your mission, you'll disembark at Deep Space Nine to play at the arcade, dine, shop, and encounter actors in alien makeup and costumes. There is an eatery called Quark's Bar that has futuristically named foods, like Glop-on-a-Stick, and in the lounge, you'll order food and drink from machines equipped with voice recognition capabilities. Showbiz Magazine often has some discount coupons for admission. Keep in mind you'll be mingling with some intense Star Trek fans who have already boasted about visiting this place for the umpteenth time. Watching them react to their surroundings with such a zealous enthusiasm is just as unsettling and entertaining as interacting with all those actors in alien costumes. **Hours:** 10-11 pm, **Admission:** $15.95, $12.95 for Nevada residents with ID. **Bus Line:** 108.

Guinness World of Records Museum

2780 Las Vegas Boulevard South (792-0640) – This museum is over 5,200 square feet. They've got loads of stuff to see, with videotapes, artifacts, and life-size replicas, all representing the records of Guinness' famous book. It's a minor stopover to be sure, but it's fun if you have time to kill. There are several publications in town that offer discount coupons for this attraction, so keep your eyes open. **Hours:** 9am-6pm, daily Admission: Adults, $4.95, Kids (12 and under), $2.95. **Bus Lines:** 301*, 302*.

Freebies

Bellagio Water Show

3600 Las Vegas Boulevard South (693-7111), www.bellagiolasvegas.com – A truly unique and attractive piece of work. Streams of water dance out of the lake to George Gershwin and Cole Porter tunes right in front of the hotel. **Hours:** 3pm-7pm every 30 minutes, 8pm-Midnight, every 15 minutes, daily. **Bus Lines:** 201*, 301*, 302*.

Fremont Street Experience

Downtown Las Vegas (800-249-3559, 678-5777), www.vegasexperience.com – The occasional traveler to Las Vegas has no doubt heard about this pedestrian promenade with overhead light show that contains over two million lights and 540,00 watts of sound. Every hour on the hour just before dusk, the overhead canopy plays a pseudo-symphony of "mystic moods" themes (birds in flight, cascading waterfalls, etc.) and dancing dice and poker chips to a string of your classic R&B songs (Aretha Franklin, the Temptations). It is impressive when you watch it the first time. The other reason to check out Fremont Street is for the free music acts. C&W Swing, Elvis imitators, ever funky-'70s retro bands and even hip '80s new wave pop acts like The English Beat and Bow Wow Wow have played here. It's pretty loose and good-natured and certainly a great value. **Hours**: Light Show – 6pm-11pm, Sun-Thurs, 6pm-Midnight, Fri-Sat, every hour on the hour. **Bus Lines**: 301*, 302* (and any bus service that takes you to the DTC terminal, from here Fremont Street is just two blocks south and it's roughly a four minute walk).

Free Keychain at the Plaza Hotel and Casino

1 S. Main Street (386-2110) – The Plaza still offers one of the best free deals in the city – a keychain with your picture on it. Just go over to the keno area and get your picture taken. It normally takes 30-45 minutes to get your keychain and you don't even have to wait around for it. Just report back in due time and they'll tell you if it's ready or not. **Hours**: It depends on how busy they are, but I once went down there with a friend at 4am and we got them without any problems. **Bus Lines**: 105, 205, 207 (these are bus lines that drop you right in front, but any bus that goes to the DTC terminal is within walking distance).

Masquerade Village at the Rio Hotel & Casino

3700 W. Flamingo Road at Valley View Boulevard (252-7777) – Visitors are invited to watch magical floats glide above the crowd to an orchestration of music, dance and celebrations. The indoor attraction features three theme parades, a cast of over 35 performers and is free to the public. **Hours**: 2pm-Midnight, Thurs-Tue. **Bus Line:** 202*.

Hard Rock Hotel & Casino

4455 Paradise Road at Harmon Road (693-5066) – The passionate opinions this casino draws are amazing. Some feel it represents their generation of anti-establishment rock rebellion. Others feel this is the ultimate in the selling out of rock & roll. Props from Mick Jagger, Elvis, and Marilyn (I know, she's not a rocker, but still a part of our morbid fascination with '50s pop culture), collectible record sleeves (a Cuban bootleg copy of Elvis' "Jailhouse Rock," and modern stuff (Sheryl Crow's gold lamé jacket), are all over this casino. While there's no denying that seeing some of this memorabilia is fascinating, the sheer artlessness of their use to lure people in and gamble their money away has such a cold-eye glint of money-consuming passion, that it's hard to ignore the paradox. Judge for yourself. **Bus Line:** 108.

Treasure Islands Pirate Battles

3300 Las Vegas Boulevard South (894-7111), www.treasureislandlasvegas.com – Hackneyed though the concept is, this is still a popular stop. The Buccaneer Bay, with the British frigate HMS Britannia, sails around Skull Point and spies the pirate ship Hispaniola unloading its booty. A pyrotechnic battle ensues as cannon and musket fire is exchanged and the sailors are thrown from their ships into the water. **Hours:** 4pm-10pm, Sun-Thurs, 4pm-11:30pm, Fri-Sat. The show "erupts" every 90 minutes. **Bus Lines:** 203, 301*, 302*.

Comedy Clubs

The Improv at Harrah's Hotel & Casino

3475 Las Vegas Boulevard South (369-5222), www.harrahsvegas.com — This city's first comedy club is still going strong. It's an offshoot of Budd Friedman's famous clubs that are so popular in New York and Los Angeles. Some of the comics who have performed here have progressed to late night television (Leno, Conan, Lettermen, etc.). **Hours:** 8pm & 10:30pm, Tue-Sun. **Admission:** $21.95 per person (drinks not included). **Bus Lines:** 202*, 301*, 302*.

The Comedy Stop at the Tropicana Hotel

3801 Las Vegas Boulevard South (739-2222), www.tropicanalv.com – A favorite comedy club for locals. There are some genuinely funny comedians who perform here and the audience is often game for anything. **Showtimes**: 8pm & 10:30pm, daily. **Admission:** Cheap fun, only $15.95 per person. Locals know to check out Showbiz Weekly, which offers discounts in its publication for the Comedy Stop, on occasion they offer two-for-one admission price specials. **Bus Lines:** 201*, 301*, 302*.

Riviera Comedy Club at the Riviera Hotel

2901 Las Vegas Boulevard South (794-9300), www.therivera.com – A satisfying surprise, not as fancy as MGM, or even the Tropicana, but on its own terms, it's pretty entertaining. There are two shows a night, each with a different comic, who fill the stage at the small Mardi Gras Center, so every seat is good because it's a rather small and cozy place. **Showtimes:** 8pm & 10pm. **Admission:** $20 per person (includes tax, gratuity and one drink). **Bus Lines:** 301*, 302*.

Low Rolling

Sure, there are a lot of things to enjoy in Las Vegas, but be honest – it's gambling that tantalizes you, and that's why most of you are here. For those who want to get a taste of gambling without draining your wallet, you are what we refer to in our fetching Vegas vernacular as a "low roller." Please don't be ashamed, I'm one too! Hey, let's face it, we want to experience that vintage Vegas feeling of rolling the dice, pulling a slot machine handle, or trying to outsmart a dealer, but that doesn't mean we have to shoot our weeks' vacation budget in one hour. Here's a quick list of popular, "low-rolling" tables my friends and I frequent.

Sahara Hotel & Casino

2535 Las Vegas Boulevard South (737-2111), www.saharahotelandcasino.com – Surprise, surprise, the Sahara Hotel is proof positive that one doesn't always need to hang downtown or in a crummy joint on the strip to find good dollar blackjack tables. On a generous night you can find anywhere from five to seven blackjack tables available 24 hours a day, daily! **Bus Lines:** 204, 301*, 302*

Slots-a-Fun

2880 Las Vegas Boulevard South (734-0410) – I'll make this place entirely your call. Slots-a-Fun is located right next to Circus Circus and is notorious for having people blow their paychecks on tables manned by some of the grimmest looking dealers you'll ever see. Still, being that you might be walking the strip and you're interested in blowing your loose change, Slots does serve a purpose. It's a little open-air joint, and the one-dollar crap and blackjack tables are located near the front of the entrance — so there's a mercurialness that offsets the dour atmosphere. If you've lost your few dollars and start feeling uncomfortable, just take a few steps toward the exit and you're back onto the sidewalk; you can pick up right where you left off and keep walking the strip. One more plus for Slots is that they offer a great ½ pound 99¢ hot dogs at the snack counter. **Bus Lines**: 301*, 302*.

El Cortez Hotel

600 Fremont Street at 6th Street (385-5200), www.elcortez.com – For you old romantics who long for gambling's suavely sinister allure of old, try "The El." Built in 1941, the El still has the atmosphere of your classic old-school hustlers trying to come out with a few bucks ahead. The odds for the dollar crap tables are good (10-1), much better than the 25¢ crap tables (2-1). The El also has a 50¢ and 10¢ roulette wheel, a game I seldom play because the odds are so low, but hey, this is chump change so it kills the time pretty well. **Bus Line**: 207.

Las Vegas Club Hotel & Casino

18 E. Fremont Street at Main Street (385-1664) – As much as I like the Las Vegas Club, I didn't think I could recommend low-rolling fun here until a friend of mine dragged me out there at 4am in the morning. It was then that I discovered every day between 3am-9am, the LV Club offers $1 blackjack tables and 25¢ crap games. Low-key and disarmingly hip, the LV Club makes even the most apprehensive beginner feel comfortable with its friendly ambience and patient attitude of the dealers and other patrons. **Bus Lines:** 108, 205.

Klondike Inn

5191 Las Vegas Boulevard South (739-9351) – A longtime favorite spot of many a traveler. The Klondike Inn is well known for their pleasant staff, terrific food, and cheap tables and slots (90% of them are nickel machines) and they have a 10¢ roulette wheel that's a blast. **Bus Lines:** 213, 301*.

Nickel Town at the Riviera Hotel & Casino

2901 Las Vegas Boulevard South (734-5110), www.theriveria.com – If you really feel like splurging, you can always head to Nickel Town at the Rivera Hotel. What makes this casino fun is that it caters to the low rent crowd (of which I am a proud member). There are more nickel slots here than anywhere on the strip and the results are a lot of cheap goodies (99¢ shrimp cocktail, 50¢ draft beer, 79¢ foot long hot dogs, and 99¢ margaritas are all offered to keep you here). Nickel Town offers some of the cheapest Vegas souvenirs on the strip from a major hotel & casino. You can normally find a coupon in Showbiz Magazine for their gift shops and get deals like three 100%, cotton T-shirts (and I mean quality T-shirts, not the kind where the print fades away after the first wash), for just $10 (regularly $9 a piece). You can also get an 11-oz. souvenir mug for just 99¢ (regularly $3), plus calendars and coasters and other Vegas related merchandise that's inexpensive. **Hours:** Slots on the Strip are *always* available 24 hours every day. **Bus Lines:** 301*, 302*.

Penny Slots

Penny slots are enjoyable for the following reasons:

1) They're cheap.
2) It's your chance to work off any obsession you might have for the slots.
3) You could win potentially big money (up to $1000).
4) You meet the strangest people who play next to you.

It's for all the reasons above that make the penny slots such a singular experience. This remains my favorite outlet for gambling. It's my chance to get rid of all the pennies I've accumulated in my coffee mug, and work off that persistent gaming bug that hassles me once every nine months. The potential "big bucks" you could win certainly doesn't rival megabucks, but I once won $250 on these slots after just depositing 75¢ worth of pennies! The people you meet while you're playing are the *real* show. I once befriended a 47-year old clove-smoking dwarf from Norway who worked at a nearby Carl's Jr. She was trying to make enough money through her jobs and the penny slots so she could start her own 900 number phone line offering tarot card readings. Oh, and she claimed to be a distant relative of that German avant-garde actress, Nastassia Kinski. I go back for the conversations.

Although many casinos offer penny slots, the two best (and most atmospheric) can be found in the popular downtown casinos (that's right, forget finding them on the strip). The **Plaza Hotel & Casino, 1 S. Main Street (386-2110), www.plazahotelcasino.com** and the **Gold Spike Inn and Casino, 400 Ogden Avenue (384-8444)**. The Gold Spike is a little more impressive because there are more penny slots (over 60) with more variety (keno, video poker, one-arm-bandits, etc.). The Plaza Hotel & Casino has sadly reduced their quantity of penny slots over the years (there are now less than a dozen) but a certain charm can still be found in this casino. It's a little classier and the people are much more friendly and talkative and they even have a progressive jackpot for pennies! For both casinos, Friday and Saturday nights can be tight. Go during a weekday morning or afternoon, and a lot more slots will be available. **Bus Lines:** Plaza Hotel — 108, 205; Gold Spike Inn — 207, 301*.

Gaming Lessons

Even though I rarely gamble, I think it's great that you can get free gaming lessons around town in some of the casinos. The most amusing ones tend to be off the beaten path in some of the smaller hotel casinos. Watching and listening to the instructors describe the nuances of the games, as well as peppering up the lessons with anecdotes of Las Vegas yore, makes for a fun afternoon. Here's a handy list of places to go for quick, free lessons.

MGM Grand Hotel

3799 Las Vegas Boulevard South (891-1111) – This major casino and resort offers the biggest platter of lessons. Roulette, Blackjack, Mini Baccarat, Craps, Poker, Caribbean Stud and Pai Gow Poker are all covered. **Hours:** On the weekdays between 9:30-3pm, Mon-Fri. in their Main Showroom. **Bus Lines:** 201*, 301*, 302*.

Riviera Hotel & Casino

2901 Las Vegas Boulevard South (734-5110), www.theriveria.com – The Riviera offers gaming lessons that are popular because the instructors strive to take the intimidation factor out of gambling, making it all pretty low-key. **Hours:** Lessons in craps, blackjack, roulette, baccarat and poker are offered between 10-2pm, Mon-Thurs. Held at the Main Casino, so you can really feel like part of the action! **Bus Lines:** 301*, 302*.

Sahara Hotel

2535 Las Vegas Boulevard South (737-2111) – The Sahara Hotel offers instruction in just two games — Craps and Blackjack, but what they lack in variety they make up for in depth. Rules of these games are not only covered, but etiquette and savvy as well. **Hours:** A table is picked on the floor to a gathering crowd and lessons are given between 11:30-1pm **Bus Lines:** 108, 204, 301*, 302*.

San Remo Resort

115 E. Tropicana Avenue at Koval Lane (739-9000) – You'll get a kick out of this one. The gaming lessons are in Japanese only. Still, if you can hang with it, you might find the animated gestures and intense delivery of the instructors entertaining. A free deck of cards will be given to those with a Japanese passport – a real cultural gas. **Hours:** Half-hour sessions are held between 4:30-11:30 pm, Mon-Fri. **Bus Lines:** 201*, 301*, 302*.

Stardust Hotel

3000 Las Vegas Boulevard South (732-6111) – Generally considered to have one of the most thorough gaming lessons in town and taught by personable professionals who have worked the floors for many years. Stardust covers virtually every aspect of casino gaming in their lessons. So thorough are the classes, it can take an entire day learning it all, so plan your schedule accordingly. **Hours:** Classes are held between 10 am-6 pm, Mon-Fri. **Bus Line:** 301*, 302*.

Las Vegas Hilton

3000 Paradise Road off Karen Avenue (732-5111) – Sessions in the fundamentals of roulette, super pan and pai gow are taught daily on the casino floor. Blackjack is taught from 11:00 am – 7:00 pm in the Learning center. **Bus Line**: 108.

Luxor Hotel & Casino

3900 Las Vegas Boulevard South (262-4000) – Taught in the main gameroom, the virginal novice to table games might enjoy this the most. The instructors here are extremely patient and friendly. It's obvious they're trying to take the intimidation factor out of table games. Sessions in roulette, super pan and pai gow. Blackjack lessons begin at noon. **Bus Lines**: 301*, 302*.

Chapter 9

Discount Cinema Houses, Theaters & Museums

The selection for discount cinema houses has thinned somewhat over the years, but we still have a few that show second run and independent pictures. As for our theater scene, well, the fact that your reaction was an incredulous "Las Vegas has a theater scene?" pretty much sums it up. There are one or two gigs worth mentioning that are both affordable and entertaining. The hidden highlights of Las Vegas, for me at least, are our unique museums, which touch on an impressive range of information (historical, ecological) and art (modern, classical, whimsical). Here is a brief rundown on some good bargains for cheap, but rewarding cinema, theater and museums.

Films

Paradise 6

3330 E. Tropicana Avenue at Pecos Road (434-8108) – A second run movie house that charges close to what they say — $2. This movie house is not without its shortcomings. The projectionists can be a little off and the floors could be cleaner, but it's so darn cheap that it's churlish to be *too* picky. Paradise 6 will not only show recent Hollywood hits that have been in circulation for a while, but small indie flicks, and an occasional foreign film, so flaws not withstanding, this is a good stop for cheap cinema. **Bus Lines:** 111, 201*.

Cinema 8

Desert Inn Road at Pecos Road (734-2124) – A recent edition to the growing family of discount theaters in Las Vegas. It's just two dollars for all shows, and there are eight screens. The selection is good — they are more or less recent hits off their peak a few months. The quality of their prints is good, and there is seldom a problem with the projectionists. Comfortable seats too. **Bus Line:** 111, 112.

UNLV International Film Series

4505 Maryland Parkway, CBCA-Room 106 (895-3547) — Here's something to cherish. An international film series that is held at the University (UNLV) every week and the films are shown free. That's right, you pay nothing. Over the years I've seen dozens of marvelous, classic films of foreign (and sometimes domestic) stock that surpasses the film viewing experience on video. The phone number listed above is UNLV's film studies department. Just call, and the receptionist will be happy to give you information on what films will be playing during your stay. **Bus Lines:** 108, 109*, 201*.

Las Vegas Drive-In

W. Carey at Rancho Road (646-3565) — This is the lone remaining Las Vegas drive-in. For many of us long-time residents, this theater retains a certain nostalgia. Built in 1960, the Las Vegas Drive-In was a terrific outlet for the whole family to see the current hit movies of the day. Remember that this was an era before suburban shopping malls with multi-plex cinema theaters, so the drive-in did excellent business throughout the '60s and '70s. Today, it's popular among Gen-Xers who like the idea of visiting an artifact of their parent's generation, allowing them to observe their surroundings with a certain level of detached irony, as well as enjoy a singular movie experience. Older locals love coming here because it offers so many memories. If you've never been to a drive-in, then you'll like it because it's certainly a unique movie-going experience and the process is easy enough. Pay your $5.50 ($3.50 on Tue.) per person at the gate, park in front of the screen of the movie of your choice, turn your radio dial to the instructed station, and enjoy. Another benefit is that you can bring your own food and drink, instead of paying those high concession stand prices at your local multiplex theater. **Hours:** The gate opens at 6 pm, Fri-Sun, 6:30 pm Mon.-Thurs. **Bus Lines:** 106, 211.

Live Theater

UNLV Theater at Artemus Ham Hall

4505 S. Maryland Parkway at Cottage Grove Circle (895-2787) – The Las Vegas theater scene, as stated earlier, is something we don't like to brag about. The few stage houses broach competency, and now and again good actors pass through, but the quality, imagination, and the inspiration of these productions are scattershot at best. UNLV can be the bright exception. Over the years, the Artemus Ham has booked guests ranging from Hal Holbrook reprising his Tony-award-winning performance in "Mark Twain Tonight," to vivid, political improvisational sketches by the San Francisco Mime Troupe. Call the box office number above and ask for information. One other highlight is the Barrick Lecture Series sponsored by local philanthropist, Marjorie Barrick. Over the years she has bankrolled such speakers as Henry Kissenger, Cokie Roberts, and Arthur Ashe. **Admission:** It depends on the play, but figure between $10-$25. The Barrick Lecture Series events are free of charge, but you have to be one of the fortunate few who can line up early at the box-office window to get first crack at the (approx. 1600) free admission tickets. **Hours:** Box Office – 10am-6pm, Mon-Fri, 10am-4pm, Sat, Closed Sun, and one hour before a scheduled show. **Bus Lines:** 109*, 213.

The Huntridge Performing Arts Theater

1208 E. Charleston Boulevard at Maryland Parkway (477-7703, 471-6700), www.Huntridgetheatre.com – This was the city's first movie house, built in 1944, and it remains an affectionately regarded historical landmark by many long-time residents. There was some concern a few years ago that the building was going to be torn down. After all, this is a city that thrives on progress, and that can shortsightedly mean tearing up everything, regardless of its cultural or historical significance. Fortunately, the uproar proved so great that the Huntridge not only was spared, it prospered. Over the years there have been some cosmetic changes, most notably in 1992 when the roof collapsed. Since then it has been remodeled and repainted. The unique interior is a grand, open space that begs for truly creative events. It's seen a lot of action of late, incuding some great alternative bands like Sugar, the Toy Dolls, Guttermouth, and the Insane Clown Posse. Even more interesting are artists of the Brit Pop Revival who've made the Huntridge a stopover for their comeback tours. The Selector, The Bodysnatchers, Bow Wow Wow, The Specials, A Flock of Seagulls (some '80s acts should stay buried) have all performed to packed houses. Best yet, many cinematic events like the wonderful "Sick and Animated Film Festival," and "Cine Vegas" have restored a certain luster to viewing films in a classic movie house. By all means, call their hotline, or check out their website to see who will be playing. **Hours:** They have no set hours for a box-office for advance ticket purchasing, you pay at the door. Admission: It varies, depending on the music acts, but I've never paid more than $20 for a ticket. **Admission:** It varies, depending on the events, but I've never paid more than $20 for a music act and the film festivals are very cheap. **Bus Lines:** 109*, 206*.

The Las Vegas Little Theatre

3844 Schiff Drive south of Spring Mountain Road (362-7996) – This theater features some pretty lowbrow productions. Slapstick British stage farces like "Noises Off," and

"Run From Your Wife" were just some of their more recent plays. A very small theater as their name suggests, but given the limitations of their budget, they do eek out an inspired production or two and the repertory actors are good. Hours: The Box Office is open one hour prior to schedule show. Admission: Check our Sunday paper for a discount coupon. Otherwise, expect to pay $12, or with your student ID, $10. **Bus Lines:** 104, 203.

The Off Broadway Theater

900 E. Karen Avenue inside the Commercial Center (737-0611) – This is a very small theater that seats just 99 people, and a lobby waiting area so small that it can barely fit a desk, let alone people who have arrived early for the show. Still, give Carl Butto — the artistic director — credit. He will always offer consistently professional pieces, even if some of the material is shopworn. The plays are generally one genre – light Broadway comedy. "A Thousand Clowns," "Never Too Late" and "Last of the Red-Hot Lovers" have been some of the latest offerings. Hours: There is no Box Office to purchase tickets in advance, you can call them at the number above and confirm reservations over the phone, or purchase tickets at the theater one hour prior to the scheduled show. Admission: $11, students with ID is $9. **Bus Line**: 109*.

Museums

Liberace Museum

1775 E. Tropicana Avenue at Spencer Road (798-5595)– This isn't a movie house or a stage show, and it's too far off the beaten path to be considered a strip highlight, but I just had to include it in this book. The Liberace Museum is a glittering piece of showmanship from a man who exemplified gaudy, Vegas splendor better than anyone. It's all here: the eerie, life-like mannequins of Liberace, the faded, yellowish newspaper clippings that represent his career, exotic cars, the diamond-studded wardrobe, and ostridge feathered cape. Finally, there is a gift shop that sells memorabilia with his likeness on everything from ashtrays to bath towels. So why not pay the $6.50 (be on the lookout for ½ price coupons in many hotel lobbies on the strip) entrance fee at the piano-shaped entrance desk, and honor the man who understood the value of kitsch before it pervaded our modern landscape? **Admission:** $6.50 for Adults, $4.95 for Seniors and Students, Free for Children under 12 years of age. **Hours:** 10am-5pm, Mon-Sat, 1pm-5pm, Sun. **Bus Line:** 201*.

Arts Factory

103 E. Charleston Boulevard at Main Street (383-3133), www.artsfactory.com – Local artist Wes Isbutt fulfilled Las Vegas' longing for a centralized arts area when he purchased an old 44,000 square–foot building (old downtown, dating back to 1944) a few years ago, off Charleston Boulevard and Main Street. The logic in this move? According to Isbutt, "the only people who are willing to fix cool old places are artists." And that's exactly what happened with the Arts Factory. Isbutt has rented the two-story building space to many galleries as well as individual artist's studios and graphics designers and there's even a central space reserved for poetry readings and avant-garde "performances." The most notable gallery is the Contemporary Arts Collective (CAC). The CAC has long been the standard bar for art with a sense of challenge and imagination and the gallery basically has an "open canvas" policy, from paintings (impressionistic, cubist), sculptures (clay to dry cotton) to performance avant-garde (metallic people moving in minute gestures like a music-box dancer). The Arts Factory is very reachable from Las Vegas Boulevard. Just drive west on Charleston for about two minutes and you'll see it on your right. **Hours:** It varies from gallery to gallery and it also depends on any special exhibits, your best bet is to call ahead for details, or check their website. **Bus Lines:** 105, 206*.

Nevada State Museum & Historical Society

700 Twin Lakes Drive south of Washington Boulevard (486-5205) – The most amusing $2 you're likely to spend while you're in town. Located near Lorenzi Park at the Sammy Davis Plaza, this witty, informative, and cleanly presented museum touches on a variety of things. Just roam from room to room and discover any number of exhibits: botanical and animal specimens of the desert, basketry of the Paiute Indians, artifacts of the early Mormon Settlers, fascinating documents and photos regarding Yucca Flats during the Atom age, the birth of the Strip — and my favorite — a brilliant postcard collection (including one that has Joe Louis as a greeter at the Moulin Rouge, which was the first African-American themed casino in the world). **Hours:** 9am – 5pm, daily. Admission: $2 for adults, free for children under 18. **Bus Line:** 208 (get off at Twin Lakes Drive and walk one block west of Lorenzi Park).

Mormon Fort

908 Las Vegas Boulevard North at Washington Avenue (486-3511) — In 1854, Las Vegas' first living, working community began when a group of Mormon settlers was sent from Salt Lake City by Bringham Young to colonize our valley. A small, adobe-brick fort was built and still stands today, making it the oldest historic landmark in Las Vegas. Unfortunately, the brutality of the heat and the roughness of the vegetation made it too difficult for these settlers, and they abandoned their Las Vegas mission within three years. Still, the remnants make for an interesting tour, it's also free. **Hours:** 8am – 3:30pm, daily. **Bus Lines:** 108, 113.

Marjorie Barrick Museum of Natural History

4505 S. Maryland Parkway (895-3381) – Located on the UNLV campus, this museum has an impressive exhibition of archaeology, anthropology and natural history of Mexico and the Southwest plus a traveling exhibit gallery. It's open year-round, and admission is free. Hours: 8am - 4:45pm, Mon-Fri., and 10am - 2pm, Sat. **Bus Lines:** 109*, 201*.

UNLV Special Collections

4505 Maryland Parkway, 4th Floor in the James Dickinson Library (895-3252) – A treasure trove filled with endlessly fascinating archival material about the history of our city. It's also a free browse and one of the most interesting stops on campus. Among the treasures: old movie posters of films shot here in the early '50s, fascinating newspaper clippings of the first gay film festival from the early '60s, blueprints of the first neon sign that went up for the Flamingo in 1949, intriguing photographs of Las Vegas through the years, and much, much more. The materials are easily available for you to browse through; just go to the PAM (pamphlets) files and look through any number of categories like architecture, gaming, major hotels and casinos, and the biographies of people who have shaped Las Vegas (Howard Hughes, Steve Wynn, Bugsy Siegel, etc.). Perhaps the most colorful category is the Film and Entertainment chapter, which is filled with amazing newspaper clippings and movie stills that have centered on our city. If you have even the slightest curiosity about Las Vegas history and you happen to be on campus, seek this place out. Self-education is seldom this fun. **Hours:** 9am-5pm, Mon-Fri. Closed for the weekends. **Bus Lines:** 108, 109*, 201*.

Elvis-A-Rama Museum

3401 Industrial Road at Spring Mountain Road (309-7200) – Well, it had to happen in this city sooner or later – an Elvis museum. Most testaments to pop cultural icons and/or phenomenons can be a little intimidating (have you ever been to a Star Trek convention?). It's not so bad here since there's an element of tongue-in-cheek to their presentation. Don't take my word for it, just check out the giant gold neon record and guitar sitting on the roof – now that's style. There are also over $3 million worth of authentic items in their inventory about the King himself. Self-proclaimed as having the largest collection of Presley's mementos outside of Graceland, you'll find it all here: cars, guitars, over 200 items of clothing, handwritten lyrics, a glorious 80-foot mural of the man himself, and (predictably) an overpriced gift shop. There's also a first rate Elvis impersonator, Tim Welsh, who performs four times a day and he's pretty good. **Hours:** Museum - 10am-6pm, daily, Impersonator Show – Noon, 2pm, 4pm and 5pm, Tue-Sun. Admission: $9.95, $7.95 for locals, but be sure to check the front desk of many hotels on the strip that offer 2-1 discount coupons. **Bus Lines:** 203, 301*, 302* (just walk one block west of the strip).

Chapter 10

The Sporting Life

Here's a brief rundown on places to go if you feel like getting a little exercise. Unfortunately, our public park system leaves something to be desired, and worse still, the best parks in town are too far away from the main heart of the city to be considered accessible. What I've listed here won't be quite so far out of your way if you're looking for athletic pursuits.

Sahara Ice Palace

953 E. Sahara Avenue at Karen Avenue inside Commercial Center (658-4991) – There are a few ice arenas in town, but this is the one closest to the strip. Don't have any skates? Not a problem, they have rentals for only $2. On weekends you can watch young Olympic hopefuls practice, which is a lot more interesting then it sounds. **Hours:** Noon-

5pm, Mon-Wed; Noon-5pm & 7:30pm-9:30pm, Thurs; Noon-5pm & 8pm-10pm, Fri; 1pm-4pm & 8pm-10pm, Sat; 1pm-4pm, Sun. Admission: $5 for adults, $4 for children under 12 years of age. **Bus Line:** 109*.

Lorenzi Park

Washington Boulevard west of Rancho Road (Parks & Recreation - 455-8200, Tennis Club – 229-4867) – Finding a tennis court on a beautiful summer night for free in this city is almost impossible. If you're looking for cheap courts, I recommend this one. For just $4 an hour, you can hit on nicely paved courts, and there's a Racquet/Pro Shop that sells everything from tennis balls to clothing apparel, plus they'll restring your rackets for a reasonable price. Another standout is their baseball field, which is very well lit. The only problem is it's often booked with little league games, but it never hurts to check. **Hours:** 7am-11pm (all public parks close at 11pm). **Bus Lines:** 106, 208.

Sunset Park

E. Sunset Road at Eastern Avenue (Parks & Recreation - 455-8200, Tennis Club - 260-9803) – Drive two miles east of the Las Vegas Strip and you'll find this park. The best pickup basketball games in town are found right here. It's not uncommon at night to see all 15 brilliantly lit courts in action. If you like tennis, Sunset has eight outdoor lighted courts that are only $3 per hour, ($5 at night). I should warn you, the main drawback to this park is the thunderous roar of the airplanes overhead (it's located very close to McCarren Airport). **Hours:** 7am-11pm, daily. **Bus Lines:** 110, 212.

Bob Baskins Park

E. Oakey Boulevard west of Rancho Drive (Parks & Recreation - 455-8200) – The best place in town for a pickup tennis match. It's no secret that the top hackers around like to come here to strike up a match with the high quality players. Four tennis courts and two backboards are provided. The courts are free, but you have to pay $1 hour for the use of the lights, which are brilliantly luminous and well worth the money. Bob Baskins also has a runner's route that goes around the park and is one of the best and most frequently used in the city. **Hours:** 7am-11pm. **Bus Line:** 205.

Las Vegas Golf Club

4300 W. Washington Drive at Decatur Boulevard (646-3003) – If you're looking for a cheap round of golf, look no further. A full round of 18 holes will cost you just $15.25, but on the weekends, every golfing Joe on a lean budget comes out here to play, so you've been warned. Throw in a lighted driving range, pro shop, coffee shop and a cocktail lounge, and the Las Vegas Club proves that an afternoon of golf can be a frugal traveler's delight. **Bus Lines:** 103. 208.

North Las Vegas Golf Club

324 E. Brooks Avenue off Cheyenne Avenue and Losee Road (633-1833) – If you are a golf fanatic and the Las Vegas Golf Club listed above is too much money for you to pay, then this is your golf course. The greens are a little bumpy, the staff is minimal, the putting green just outside the pro shop is the practice facility and the pro shop is limited to just a few products. However, it's very affordable –

just $6 ($7.50 on the weekends) for a round of (9-holes) golf. The friendly attitude of the golfers who frequent this place, the overall low-key atmosphere of the staff and the lack of a crowd goes a long way in erasing any intimidating environment for the novice golfer to learn the sport. **Bus Line:** 218, (it's a long bus ride — you're better off taking a car. Just head north on I-15, exit on Cheyenne Avenue, turn left, head toward Losee Road, make another left and then a right when you hit Brooks Road – phew!).

Scandia Family Fun Center

2900 Sirius Avenue off Rancho Drive (364-0070) – Miniature golf, go-carts, boats, batting cages, if you're in the mood to have a go at disarming, innocent fun in Las Vegas, Scandia is your best bet. It's located near I-15, it's in the heart of town, just off Sahara Avenue. The mini golf course is the most fun because it's filled with imaginative trimmings — windmills, moats, mini-rollercoasters, etc. Okay, so this might not be the most arduous athletic pursuit, but it's still affordable fun. Admission: All-day pass $15.95, Free for children under 5 years of age. **Hours:** 10am-10pm, Mon-Thurs, 10-11 pm, Fri.-Sat., Closed Sun. **Bus Line:** 401 (and walk three blocks south).

Not so much a sport activity as a spectator sport, the **Las Vegas Stars** is our minor-league baseball team. While they won't overwhelm you with any kind of supernatural athleticism, they can offer a low-key enjoyment of sorts. The games are played at **Cashman Field, 850 N. Las Vegas**

Boulevard (798-7825). It's fairly inexpensive, costing you as little as $7 per person for the night. It's also a pretty good team, so good that over the years more than 135 former Las Vegas Stars' players went into the major ranks. Best of all is the atmosphere, which is refreshingly low-key. With any luck, the players will even autograph your program for you after the game. If a certain player makes his name later on, you have yourself a collectible. **Bus Line:** 113*, 208.

Index

D

E

F

Notes

Other Books by JASI

The Best of Central California: Main Roads and Side Trips, *Bob Carter*

Award-winning writer Bob Carter covers everything from missions to wineries along highways 1, 101, 99, 395, and 14. Includes trips off the beaten path.

$14.95, 303 pages, ISBN 1881409104

The Best of Orange County California: A Guide to Scenic, Recreational and Historical Attractions, Second edition, *Gregory Lee*

This guidebook includes restaurants, beaches, museums, well-known theme parks and lesser-known recreational gems.

$16.95, 304 pages, ISBN 1881409260

The Brewpub Explorer of the Pacific Northwest, Second edition, *Hudson Dodd, Matthew Latterell and Ina Zucker*

This fully updated edition is the perfect companion to help readers explore the multitude of micro-breweries in Washington, Oregon and British Columbia.

$16.95, 256 pages, ISBN 1881409252

California's Gold Rush Country: A Guide to the Best of the Mother Lode, *Barbara Braasch*

From assay offices to tailing wheels and antique fairs to wine tours, this book is packed with travel tips and "don't miss" attractions for all seasons.

$14.95, 203 pages, ISBN 1881409147

Discover Washington with Kids, Second edition, *Rosanne Cohn & Suzanne Monson*

This guide explores both familiar landmarks and hidden treasures with kid appeal in Washington State.

$16.95, 272 pages, ISBN 1881409228

Discover the Southwest with Kids, *Mary Vasudeva*

From ancient Indian cities to frontier forts, from national parks to museums, festivals and magical out-of-the way places, this is an indispensable guide.

$16.95, 256 pages, ISBN 1881409244

Discover the Poconos with Kids: A Guide for Families, *Marynell K. Strunk*

Covers entertainment, lodging, activities and sports, festivals, and more.

$12.95, 168 pages, ISBN 1881409201

The Essential San Juan Islands Guide,
Third edition, *Marge and Ted Mueller*

This new edition covers dining, lodging, shopping, boating, bicycling, camping, and special festivals.

$16.95, 304 pages, ISBN 1881409287

The Pitiful Gardener's Handbook: Successful Gardening in Spite of Yourself
Connie Eden & Tracy Cheney

This easy to understand handbook will appeal to anyone looking to make the right time- and money-saving decisions to achieve happy gardening results.

$12.95, 176 pages, ISBN 1881409236

Oregon's Coast: A Guide to the Best Family Attractions from Astoria to Brookings
Carolyn & David Gabbe

Contains information on beachcombing, dune buggy riding, tidepooling, and whalewatching.

$11.95, 192 pages, ISBN 1881409007

The Seattle Super Shopper: The Savvy Shopper's Guide to the Greater Puget Sound Area,
Ninth edition, *Mac Johnston and Rebecca Stanton*

The latest and greatest revised best-seller of information on over 1,500 Puget Sound area places selling brand-names at rock-bottom prices.

$16.95, approx. 256 pages, ISBN 1881409309

Spokane: The Complete Guide to the Hub of the Island Northwest, *M.E. Buckham*

This extensive guide to the Lilac City tells where to stay, shop, eat and play in and around this region.

$14.95, 256 pages, ISBN 1881409139

Stepping Out in Seattle, Second edition,
Mandy Johnston

This guide makes it easy for singles, couples and friends to plan playtime together in the Emerald City.

$12.95, 192 pages, ISBN 188140921X

About the Author

Michael Toole was born to write a travel guide. He started life out as a military brat (he was born in an Army Hospital in Okinawa, Japan) and knew about crowded airports, lost luggage, and dodgy cab drivers before he could walk.

Since the mid-1970s when his family settled in Las Vegas, Toole has been a resident of the city. In this period, he was productive enough to acquire a couple of degrees (B.A. in Film - 1993, B.A. in Communications Studies - 1994) from the University of Nevada, Las Vegas. Michael also took advantage of the money he saved from many summer jobs to take trips all over North America and Europe. He appreciates the value of a budget room and a reasonably priced pint of lager.

Michael has contributed to publications as diverse as the Time Out Travel Publications series and the Turner Classic Movies website. He spent time as the Research Coordinator for the Las Vegas Advisor, which gave him good training in budget hunting for his book. He is single (any takers?) with no pets.

Contributing photographer Ginger Bruner is a very busy woman. In addition to her work as a photographer she is also a tuba player in a punk polka band, a professional circus clown, a popular radio personality in Las Vegas and a tennis player with a mean topspin serve. Her contributions to this book include the photos of the author on the back cover and on this page, as well as the cover shots of the wedding chapel and the showgirl.